Ancient Peoples and Places

MALTA

General Editor

DR GLYN DANIEL

Ancient Peoples and Places

MALTA

J. D. Evans

97 PHOTOGRAPHS

33 LINE DRAWINGS

2 MAPS AND A TABLE

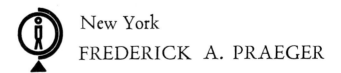

New York

FREDERICK A. PRAEGER

THIS IS VOLUME ELEVEN IN THE SERIES

Ancient Peoples and Places

GENERAL EDITOR: DR GLYN DANIEL

ALREADY PUBLISHED   1   PERU
G. H. S. Bushnell

2   THE SCYTHIANS
T. Talbot Rice

3   SICILY BEFORE THE GREEKS
L. Bernabò Brea

4   DENMARK BEFORE THE VIKINGS
O. Klindt-Jensen

5   THE LOW COUNTRIES
S. J. De Laet

6   THE CELTS
T. G. E. Powell

7   THE ETRUSCANS
Raymond Bloch

8   EARLY CHRISTIAN IRELAND
Máire and Liam de Paor

9   WESSEX BEFORE THE CELTS
J. F. S. Stone

10   JAPAN BEFORE BUDDHISM
J. E. Kidder Jr

BOOKS THAT MATTER   *Published in the United States of America
in 1959 by Frederick A. Praeger, Inc.,
Publishers, 15 West 47th Street,
New York 36, N.Y.
All rights reserved
Library of Congress Catalog Card Number: 59-8141
Printed in Great Britain*

CONTENTS

LIST OF ILLUSTRATIONS 7

FOREWORD 15

INTRODUCTION: THE DISCOVERY
OF MALTA'S PREHISTORIC PAST 17

I THE MAKING OF MALTA 31

II THE EARLIEST MALTESE 39

TABLE OF PREHISTORIC CULTURE
IN THE MALTESE ISLANDS 42

III TEMPLES AND TOMBS 84

IV RELIGION AND
LIFE IN ANCIENT MALTA 135

V THE DESTROYERS 168

APPENDIX I 189

APPENDIX II 191

APPENDIX III 193

BIBLIOGRAPHY 194

SOURCES OF ILLUSTRATIONS 196

THE PLATES 197

NOTES ON THE PLATES 245

INDEX 253

5

ILLUSTRATIONS

PLATES   1   Interior of Għar Dalam

2   Aerial photograph of Ta Ħaġrat, Mġarr

3   Terracotta model of a temple

4   Chamber in larger building, Ta Ħaġrat, Mġarr

5   Façade of the southern temple, Ġgantija

6   The Ġgantija from the south

7   Painting of first chamber on right in the southern temple, Ġgantija, done in 1827

8   Photograph of the same chamber

9   Second chamber on left in the southern building, Ġgantija

10   Northern temple of the Ġgantija from the entrance

11   Rear wall of the Ġgantija

12   Façade of the Ħaġar Qim temples

13   Aerial view of Ħaġar Qim

14   First chamber on the right at Ħaġar Qim

15   Second chamber on the right at Ħaġar Qim

16   Corridor with altars and pitted slabs, Ħaġar Qim

17   Aerial view of the Mnajdra temples

18   Passage between chambers, southern temple, Mnajdra

PLATES 19 Elaborately decorated entrance, southern temple, Mnajdra

20 Entrance to chamber in walls, Mnajdra

21 First chamber on right, northern temple, Mnajdra

22 First chamber on the right, southern temple, Mnajdra

23 First chamber on left, western temple, Tarxien

24 Originals of spiral carvings, Tarxien

25 Rear chamber of western temple, Tarxien

26 First room of middle temple, Tarxien

27 Cutting through floors, eastern temple, Tarxien

28 Second chamber on left, middle temple, Tarxien

29 Carved hall, Hal Saflieni

30 Elaborately carved chamber, Hal Saflieni

31 Hall with painted ceiling, Hal Saflieni

32 Entrance to tombs 1 and 2, Xemxija

33 Interior of tomb 1, Xemxija

34, 35 Potsherds with impressed decoration, Għar Dalam

36 Flat bottomed bowls from the Żebbuġ tombs

37, 38 Phase IC pots

39 Biconical bowl from Tarxien

40 'Hanging bowl' from Hal Saflieni

PLATES   41, 42   Studded bowls from Tarxien

43   Biconical jar from Tarxien

44   Carinated bowl from Tarxien

45   Large storage jar from Tarxien

46   'Amphora' from Tarxien

47   Storage jar from Tarxien

48   Head of limestone statue, tomb 5, Żebbuġ

49   Headless standing figure from Ħaġar Qim

50   Headless standing figure from Hal Saflieni

51, 52   Alabaster figurines from Hal Saflieni

53   Seated limestone figure, Ħaġar Qim

54   Seated limestone figure in gown, Ħaġar Qim

55, 56   Two limestone heads, Hal Saflieni

57   The 'Sleeping Lady', Hal Saflieni

58, 59, 60   'Priest' from Tarxien

61   Terracotta female figure from Tarxien

62   Figure stuck with splinters of shell, Tarxien

63   Pigtailed limestone statuette, Ħaġar Qim

64   Deformed female figure in clay, Mnajdra

65   The 'Venus of Malta' from Ħaġar Qim

66, 67, 68   Stone heads from Tarxien

69   Head in stalactite, Tarxien

70   Pigtailed head, Tarxien

71   Terracotta lizard, Tarxien

72   Animal-head handle, Għar Dalam

73   Bird between horns modelled on sherd, Tarxien

9

PLATES   74   Sherd with crested birds in flight, Ġgantija
         75   Shallow plate with cattle and goats, Hal Saflieni
         76   Relief-carving of shrine, Mnajdra
         77   Limestone model of shrine, Ta Haġrat, Mġarr
         78   Slab with oculus spirals, Haġar Qim
         79   Floral 'altar', Haġar Qim
         80   Beads and pendants, Hal Saflieni
         81   Shell buttons and pendant, Hal Saflieni
         82   Axe-pendants, Hal Saflieni
         83   Implements of obsidian, Tarxien
         84   Bead inlaid with gold and gems, Tarxien
         85   Potsherds and pebble incised with signs
         86   Part of limestone basin, Haġar Qim
         87   Model niche with phalli, Tarxien
         89   Stylized idol, Cremation cemetery, Tarxien
     88, 90   Decorated pots, Cremation cemetery, Tarxien
         91   Stylized idol, Cremation cemetery, Tarxien
         92   'Dolmen' near Musta, Malta
         93   Defensive wall, Borġ in-Nadur
         94   Footed bowl, Borġ in-Nadur
         95   Bowl with axe-handle, Borġ in-Nadur
     96, 97   Decorated pots from Bahrija

FIGURES 1 *Map of the Maltese Islands, p. 19*

2 *Pottery shapes of phase IB, p. 49*

3 *Pottery shapes of phase IC, p. 53*

4 *Pottery of phase IC, p. 55*

5, 6 *Potsherds from the Zebbuġ tombs, pp. 57, 59*

7 *Flint blades from the Zebbuġ tombs, p. 61*

8 *Shell and bone beads from the Zebbuġ tombs, p. 63*

9 *Pottery shapes of phase ID, p. 69*

10 *Pottery of phase ID from the Xemxija tombs, p.71*

11 *Pottery shapes of phase IE, p. 79*

12 *Long flint blades from the Tarxien temples, p. 83*

13 *Plans of the earlier types of temple-units, p. 87*

14 *Plans of tombs 5 and 6 at Xemxija, p. 88*

15 *Plans of tombs 1 and 2 at Xemxija, p. 89*

16 *Plans and sections of tombs 4 and 5 at Zebbuġ, p. 93*

17 *Plans of the later types of temple-units, p. 97*

18 *Plan of the Tarxien temples, p. 104*

19 *Reconstruction of fragments of model façade from Tarxien, p. 114*

20 *Reconstruction of Tarxien façade (after Ceschi), p. 115*

21 *Stylized clay heads, p. 141*

22 *Sketch of a 'dancing girl', Tarxien, p. 147*

23 *Part of procession of animals, Tarxien, p. 149*

24 *Stylized figurine of bovid, Hal Saflieni, p. 149*

25 *Figures of animals, Tarxien, p. 150*

FIGURES   26   *Stylized figurine of bird, Hal Saflieni, p. 151*

27   *Stone amulet, Tarxien, p. 155*

28   *Sherd of channelled ware from the Ġgantija, p. 161*

29   *Bead from Hal Saflieni, p. 161*

30   *Pottery shapes of phase IIA, p. 170*

31   *Plan and sections of 'dolmen' at Ta Hammut, p. 174*

32   *Plan showing relation of defensive wall to temple at Borġ in-Nadur, p. 181*

33   *Pottery shapes of phase IIB, p. 183*

34   *Reconstruction of Mycenean chalice from Borġ in-Nadur, p. 186*

35   *Pottery shapes of phase IIC, p. 187*

To the People of Malta and Gozo

Foreword

THE MALTESE ISLANDS have known two periods of especial cultural splendour during their long history. One, the better-known, was during the centuries when they were the base and headquarters of the Knights of St John; the other, more remote, goes back to the far-off time when men first landed and made a home in these tiny 'isles of the sea'. There they found the peace and leisure to create a civilization, to build great megalithic temples, to hollow out huge catacombs in the living rock and to elaborate an art and sculpture unequalled in Western Europe in their time and for many centuries later.

In this book I have attempted to summarize what we know of this first civilization of Malta—the coming of the colonists, where they came from, and the various stages their culture passed through on the islands—and to describe the main products of their skill and faith. Finally, I have dealt briefly with the various people who succeeded them in Malta when they finally vanished about 1450 B.C., and who occupied the islands during the remaining centuries of their prehistory.

The text embodies conclusions (already published in scattered articles) which I arrived at whilst working on a Survey of Prehistoric Malta, for the Royal University of Malta, the full results of which will be published shortly in the form of a corpus of the prehistoric monuments and material.

Many of my conclusions about the origins, development and chronology of the first Maltese civilization and its successors are based on comparisons with Sicilian material. While it is possible to read this book on its own, the reader would undoubtedly find it useful to have Dr L. Bernabò Brea's book *Sicily before the Greeks*, in the same series, at hand to consult.

My debts of gratitude are many and heavy. First of all to the Advisory Committee of the Archaeological Survey of Malta and its Chairman, Professor J. Manché, for the opportunity to work in Malta and for many kindnesses while there; to the Directors of the Valletta Museum (now the National Museum), past and present, Chev. Dr J. G. Baldacchino and Mr C. G. Zammit, for the free run of the Museum and for much help at all times; to the staff of the Museum and to various voluntary helpers. I also wish to thank Mr J. B. Ward Perkins and Professor Stuart Piggott for their help and encouragement, as also Dr L. Bernabò Brea, not only for the help which he has extended from time to time, but also for the continuous inspiration of his own magnificent work in Sicily and the Lipari islands which has so great a bearing on Malta.

Finally, I should like to thank Dr Glyn Daniel for his help and encouragement from my undergraduate days onwards, but especially for his infinite patience at the delays which have attended the production of the following pages.

J. D. E.

Introduction: The Discovery of Malta's Prehistoric Past

THE REMAINS of the huge megalithic buildings erected by the earliest inhabitants of Malta and Gozo must always have attracted the attention of the later inhabitants of these islands, and invited speculation about their early history. In spite of this, and in spite of the fact that the more imposing of them are mentioned by writers about the islands from the mid-17th century onwards, knowledge of Malta's remote past grew slowly. Excavation began only in the second quarter of the 19th century. In the succeeding decades a number of the larger and more prominent groups of ruins were cleared, though unfortunately this work was carried out so casually and amateurishly (in the bad sense) that little of scientific value was learned, and even that little rarely published. A better state of affairs was achieved only in the present century, largely through the devoted work of excavation and publication carried out over more than a quarter of a century by Sir Themistocles Zammit. Since 1950 a thorough study of the accumulated material has been made in the course of the Prehistoric Survey, which has for the first time made fully intelligible the role of Malta in the prehistoric development of the Western Mediterranean.

When Quintinus Haeduus, writing his *Descriptio insulae Melitae* in the 16th century, made mention of some ruins near the great bay of Marsaxlokk, on the south-east coast of Malta (which he identified with those of a Temple of Hercules, said by the Greek geographer Ptolemy to exist in Malta), he may have had in mind some important Bronze Age ruins now known as Borġ in-Nadur, but it is not possible to be certain of

Fig. 1 (25)
Plate 93

17

this. The first certain references to prehistoric remains in the Maltese islands occur in the work called *Della Descrittione di Malta,* which was written by the Commendatore G. F. Abela, an official of the Knights of St John in Malta, and published in 1647. A second edition of this work edited and annotated by Count Ciantar, appeared in 1772. A few years after this the Maltese islands were visited by Jean Houel, engraver to King Louis XVI of France, who in due course published an account of his observations in the fourth volume of his work called *Voyage pittoresque des isles de Sicile, de Malte, et de Lipari* which appeared in 1787. Houel gives descriptions of some of the chief visible prehistoric remains, accompanying them with engravings made by himself, which are of great interest as showing the appearance of these monuments in the late 18th century, before any had been excavated.

Fig. 1 (11)

Plates 5–11
Fig. 17 (1, 2)

The first of the monuments to be excavated was one which is still in some ways the most impressive of all the remains, the complex known as the Ġgantija, near the village of Xagħra in Gozo. Operations were begun here in 1827, at the instigation of Col. Otto Bayer, who was in charge of the island at that time. A short description of the monument was published in the same year by L. Mazzara in Paris, under the quaint title of *Temple anté-Diluvien des Giants,* and in 1829 a short note with some illustrations appeared in the *Archaeologia,* the publication of the Society of Antiquaries of London. However, a much fuller and better description, by Alberto de la Marmora, was published in 1836. The eminently picturesque remains of the Ġgantija became a favourite subject for artists in the second quarter of the 19th century, and thus we have several sets of paintings and drawings which are important because they show many details of the internal arrangement of the buildings which have since been destroyed.

Plates 7, 8

Fig. 1 (14)
Plates 12–16

In 1839 the ruins of Haġar Qim, another big temple-complex, were excavated with funds supplied by the then

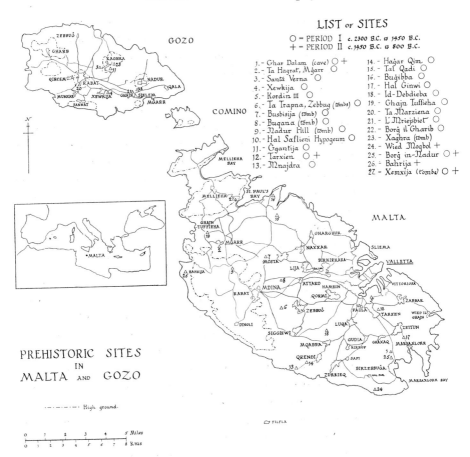

LIST of SITES

○ = PERIOD I c. 2300 B.C. *a* 1450 B.C.
+ = PERIOD II c. 1450 B.C. *a* 800 B.C.

1.- Ghar Dalam (cave) ○ +
2.- Ta Ħagrat, Mġarr ○
3.- Santa Verna ○
4.- Xewkija ○
5.- Kordin III ○
6.- Ta Trapna, Żebbuġ (tombs) ○
7.- Busbisija (tomb) ○
8.- Buqana (tomb) ○
9.- Nadur Hill (tomb) ○
10.- Hal Saflieni Hypogeum ○
11.- Ġgantija ○
12.- Tarxien ○ +
13.- Mnajdra ○

14.- Ħaġar Qim ○
15.- Tal Qadi ○
16.- Buġibba ○
17.- Hal Ġinwi ○
18.- Id-Debdieba ○
19.- Għajn Tuffieħa ○
20.- Ta Marziena ○
21.- L' Mriejsbiet ○
22.- Borġ il Gharib ○
23.- Xagħra (tomb) ○
24.- Wied Moqbol +
25.- Borġ in-Nadur ○ +
26.- Bahrija +
27.- Xemxija (tombs) ○ +

PREHISTORIC SITES
IN
MALTA AND GOZO

.—.—.—.— High ground.

0 1 2 3 4 5 Miles
0 1 2 3 4 5 6 7 8 Kms

Fig. 1 Map of the Maltese Islands, showing the main sites

Governor of Malta, Sir H. Bouverie, but only a very inadequate report was published (in *Archaeologia*) by J. G. Vance, who supervised the work. During the next year, 1840, the nearby site of Mnajdra was excavated, following the completion of the work at Ħaġar Qim, but this time no report appeared at all.

Fig. 1 (13)
Plates 17–22

19

Plate 93

The work of discovery, begun in this not very auspicious manner, languished during most of the remainder of the century, with the exception of some excavations carried out by Dr A. A. Caruana, the librarian of the Royal Malta Library to which the Museum was at that time attached. In 1881 he partially cleared the huge Bronze Age defences at Borġ in-Nadur, but unfortunately published no report on the work. Two megalithic buildings were excavated on Kordin Hill during 1892, and Caruana reported on this work, giving a plan of the buildings, in the *Archaeological Journal* for 1896. He also undertook some new work at Ħaġar Qim, and published a short report on it with a plan of the monument.

Caruana's *Report on the Phoenician and Roman Antiquities* (1882) and a later work of his on ancient Malta published in 1899 deal briefly with the megalithic monuments, but without contributing anything fresh, and the same is true of a work by C. Vassallo on the ancient monuments of the Maltese islands which was first published in 1851 and again in a revised edition in 1876. The amazing megalithic architecture of Malta and Gozo was by now, however, becoming widely known and arousing considerable interest among antiquaries and historians of architecture. Accounts of the Maltese monuments appear in various general works published during the later 19th century, as, for instance the great *Histoire de l'Art dans l'Antiquité,* and in James Fergusson's world study of megalithic structures called *Rude Stone Monuments.* Still nothing was known with certainty about their age, but scarcely anyone dreamed that they were prehistoric. Most writers were quite happy to assume that they had been built by the Phoenicians, though no similar buildings could be found either in their homeland or any other territory which they inhabited. It was hardly even surmised that they might belong to a remote nameless race far more ancient than the historical Phoenicians. Fergusson, however, rejected the idea of Phoenicians because of the lack of parallels, and was inclined to look for their origin in the megalithic monuments of North Africa.

Altogether the record of work on the prehistoric monuments of Malta and Gozo during the 19th century is a melancholy one. The general standard is much below that of the work done during the same period on the geology and palaeontology of the islands, which involved the excavation of caves, in which rich deposits of animal bones deposited during the quaternary period were found. One of these, Għar Dalam, also produced important remains of the activity of prehistoric man in its upper levels. The excavation and study of the remains, especially tombs and their contents, dating from the real Phoenician (or Punic) and Roman periods, was also on the whole much better done than that on the remains of the prehistoric period. This may be partly accidental, but it must also be due in part to the fact that the former fitted into the pattern of known and mapped civilizations, and so lent themselves more easily to description and classification, than the outlandish megaliths, though these were generally considered to belong to about the same period.

In so far as the megalithic monuments were concerned, the 19th-century excavations meant simply the clearance of the accumulated earth and stones which had transformed the buildings into mere mounds of rubble from which protruded the tops of large stones. Once exposed, the buildings were left to decay, without any adequate record having been made of them; and the material found in them, with the exception of a few choice or exceptional pieces, was thrown away or lost without any thought of publication. In 1851 indeed, Sir Charles Newton collected 'two cartloads' of pottery at Ħaġar Qim and sent them to the Valletta Museum, but in 1902, all the pottery from this site was contained in two baskets which had just been discovered in a lumber-room above the Public Library in Valletta. A much greater quantity of material than this must have been found in the original excavations, of which

Fig. 1 (1)
Plate 1

Plates 7, 8

21

there is not even so much record. As a result little or no progress was made during the 19th century in the serious study of the megalithic temples and the culture which produced them. At the end of the century most writers were still ascribing them to the Phoenicians.

A herald of better things was the excellent work done by the German scholar Albert Mayr in the closing years of the 19th century. Mayr made several visits to Malta, and in 1901 pub-lished a fine monograph, 'Die vorgeschichtlichen Denkmäler von Malta', in which he gave the first adequate account of the prehistoric buildings then known, and made a brilliant attempt to assess their context and significance in the prehistory of the Mediterranean. A revised and shortened version of this work was translated into English by Princess Battenberg and appeared in 1908. Mayr also published another account of the Maltese megalithic culture, incorporating new material, in a work called *Die Insel Malta im Altertum,* which appeared in 1909 and which covered also the Punic and Roman periods.

Fig. 1 (10)
Plates 29, 31

In 1902 a major discovery was made when the labyrinth of rock-cut halls and chambers now known as the Hypogeum of Hal Saflieni came to light. The circumstances of the find were most unfortunate. Some houses were being built on the land above the Hypogeum, and a workman who was engaged on hewing out one of the bell-shaped water-tanks with which every Maltese house is provided accidently broke through into one of the chambers. The builder finished his houses, using the underground chambers as a convenient dump for his rubbish, and only then informed the Government of the discovery. A committee was then formed and it was decided to investigate the monument. Fr E. Magri was put in charge of the excavations, which continued for some time, but Magri then had to leave Malta and died at Susa in 1907 without having published a report. His notes could not be found, and it seemed as though the old sad story was about to repeat itself. Fortunately, how/ ever, at this point the continuation of the work was entrusted to Sir Themistocles, or, as he then was, Dr Themistocles Zammit.

Zammit was a man of great and varied abilities, and his activities ranged over many fields, but perhaps his greatest and most enduring achievement was his contribution to Maltese archaeology. As Director of the Malta Museum he, by his work during the following year, laid the solid foundations of our present knowledge of Maltese prehistory. In this activity he had many helpers, both Maltese and British, but it was he who during the rest of his life formed the nodal point of all work concerned with Maltese antiquities.

The work on the Hypogeum was completed under Zammit's direction, and in 1911 a full description of the monument by him was published, along with a plan. The following year a study of the small finds and human remains prepared by him in collaboration with T. E. Peet and H. N. Bradley made its appearance. Already in 1910 Professor N. Tagliaferro had published an important paper on the pottery found in the Hypogeum up to that time. Apart from the excavation of the Hypogeum, however, much other work was carried out in the decade or so before 1914. In the first year of the century Fr Magri had excavated and published an account of some megalithic remains at Xewkija, in Gozo, while between 1908 and 1911 Dr Thomas Ashby, Director of the British School at Rome, carried out with the assistance of T. E. Peet a series of important excavations on various prehistoric sites in Malta and Gozo, some previously excavated, such as Ħaġar Qim and Mnajdra, others, such as Kordin South and Santa Verna in Gozo, newly discovered. Their results were duly published in the *Papers* of the British School at Rome.   *Fig. 1 (5, 3)*

Despite all the work carried out in the years preceding the First World War, however, it had not proved possible to

Fig. 1 (12)
Plates 23–28
Fig. 18

subdivide the prehistoric period in any satisfactory way. Peet had indeed suggested tentatively that some types of pottery might be earlier than others, and in 1910 he had himself conducted a trial excavation at the settlement of Bahrija, which had produced pottery quite unlike that normally found in the temples. In 1914, however, Zammit began excavations in some newly discovered megalithic ruins at Tarxien which were to prove epoch-making in many ways. Work continued at Tarxien regularly each year until 1919, and a complex of structures covering a considerable area was laid bare. Zammit published full reports on his work, first in *Archaeologia*, and later in his book called *Prehistoric Malta*. These provide the only full and complete record we have of the excavation of any major megalithic monument in the Maltese islands. In one area of the Tarxien ruins a cemetery of cremation graves was found in urns, accompanied by a strange and unfamiliar type of pottery. The stratum containing these, which showed clear signs of heavy burning, was separated by 3 ft of sterile soil from the material which lay on the floors of the temple below, and which was of the type normally found in the temples. It was clear from this that the Tarxien temples had been re-used, when already in ruins and deserted by their original builders, by a later, but still prehistoric, folk for their own purposes, which were quite different from those for which the buildings had been designed. It was thus clear that the temple-builders had been succeeded by at least one other prehistoric culture before the islands came into the half-light of protohistory with the arrival of the Carthaginians. Also, since among the remains found in the cremation cemetery were some simple copper daggers, axes and awls, whilst no metal objects had been found among the remains of the temple people, it seemed reasonable to see in the latter the Neolithic inhabitants of the Maltese islands and in the former the Bronze Age culture.

This was certainly a great advance, though it still remained impossible to account satisfactorily for the origins of either culture, or to date either of them with any certainty. Most authorities, however, were inclined, following current theories of the North African origin of the 'Mediterranean race', and the rather vague North African connections of the megaliths, to see the temple-builders as coming originally from this large and at that time archaeologically little-known territory. Subsequent research has not confirmed this theory. The North African megaliths seem all to be very late, and it is now possible to find much better analogies to some of the Maltese Neolithic material in nearby Sicily. In the case of the Tarxien Bronze Age culture, Zammit was able to point to some striking general similarities with the Early Bronze Age cultures of the Eastern Mediterranean, and to suggest that they had come originally from this direction. In general it may be said that Zammit's parallels and deductions were quite valid, though it has been possible subsequently to demonstrate in much more detail the way in which the culture was formed and in which it ultimately reached the Maltese islands. Zammit favoured dates of about 3000 B.C. for the Neolithic temple-culture, and about 2000 B.C. for the Tarxien Bronze Age culture, but these were little more than guesswork. The first was based on currently popular datings for the European Neolithic in general, and the second on the dating of the Early Bronze Age in the Eastern Mediterranean. Both have subsequently been shown to be considerably too high.

In the years between the two World Wars a fair amount of new work was carried out in Malta, but the results were generally disappointing in so far as they produced no real advances in the classification and dating of the Maltese material. In 1945 nothing more was known with certainty about these subjects than in 1918. Nevertheless, much new material was accumulated, which would find its place when the problem was seriously tackled as a whole. During and just after the

First World War several minor megalithic monuments were excavated, such as those at Xrobb il-Għaġin and Id-Debdieba, whilst in the 'twenties two most important excavations took place at the sites of Borġ in-Nadur, near Birzebbuġa, and Mġarr respectively. The excavations at Borġ in-Nadur were carried out by Dr Margaret Murray in several campaigns between 1922 and 1927 and the results were published in the three volumes of her *Excavations in Malta* (*1923–9*). Although the excavations were entirely confined to the ruins of a Neolithic temple-complex which lies behind the huge Bronze Age wall mentioned earlier, the material recovered consisted over-whelmingly of Bronze Age pottery of a new type, which

Plates 94, 95

differed equally from that found by Zammit at Tarxien and that earlier discovered by Peet at Bahrija. The temple-ruins, lying as they did in the area enclosed and defended by the wall, had been intensively re-used by the Bronze Age settlers for domestic purposes, such as grinding and storing grain. Despite the Neolithic temple, and the relatively small amount of Neolithic pottery and other material it contained, Borġ in-Nadur remains the type-site of a phase of the Bronze Age.

Fig. 1 (2)
Plates 2, 4
Fig. 13 (1, 2)

Even more important were the excavations carried out at the megalithic temple of Ta Haġrat (The Stone Heap) near the village of Mġarr, which has proved to be a most vital site for the understanding of the development of the temple-culture (as we may call the period of the builders of the megalithic monuments) in Malta. These excavations were under the general direction of Zammit, who, however, was so busy at this time that the actual supervision had to be entrusted to volunteer helpers. A short report on the excavations, which were carried out at intervals between 1923 and 1926, was prepared by Zammit and published in the first issue of the Museum *Bulletin.* Unfortunately on this occasion he completely mis-understood the significance of the site, which he interpreted as showing a late stage of the Neolithic culture, and a phase of 'transition to the Bronze Age', whereas it is now abundantly clear that its importance lies in the evidence which it provides about two of the earliest stages of the temple-culture.

The work at Mġarr was the last excavation of major importance undertaken between the wars, though other minor sites were excavated, including the Tal Qadi temple, and the small temple at Buġibba, on the north coast of Malta, which produced some charming and unique carvings representing fish. A number of small-scale investigations were also made at the older sites, and occasional small tombs belonging to the prehistoric period were investigated as they were accidentally discovered. Only one large-scale attempt was made at a general study and evaluation of the prehistoric material during the early 'thirties by the Italian archaeologist Ugolini, but his study and its main conclusions, namely that in the Maltese Neolithic might be sought the 'origin of Mediterranean civilization', were vitiated by political bias. Nevertheless, it is interesting to note that in 1933 it was still possible for such a claim to be made without bringing immediate ridicule upon its author. Apart from its immediate aim as part of the Fascist government's campaign of political infiltration in Malta, the idea was the counterpart of the Nazi prehistorians' search for the origins of culture in the backwoods of North-West Europe. Both had their origin, like some more serious archaeological thinking of the time, in a violent reaction away from the theory, whose basic principle is now almost universally accepted as axiomatic, that all the major steps in the attainment of civilization were taken in the Near East, and first affected Europe largely as a result of diffusion from that region. What made possible the large measure of success which this reaction enjoyed for a time was the vagueness of the time-scale for prehistoric Europe. Great latitude was often possible in assigning dates in years to any particular culture.

For the Maltese cultures this remained the case until the last

Fig. 1 (15, 16)

few years. Zammit's dates for the Neolithic and Bronze Age were mere guesses, based on little positive evidence, and each of these periods almost certainly covered a long period of time and should be capable of subdivision. So much was obvious, but it was not until after the end of the Second World War that it became possible to see what could be done along these lines. Through the influence of the late Dr Ifor Evans, it was arranged that a grant should be made by the Inter-University Council for Higher Education in the Colonies to the Royal University of Malta, with which he was associated, to finance a survey of the existing materials for the study of Maltese prehistory, both the monuments and the collections of the Valletta Museum (now the National Museum), with a view to their ultimate publication in the form of a complete corpus. A committee was formed to administer this grant, with the Rector and Vice-Chancellor, Professor J. Manché, as Chairman, and including among its members the then Director of the Museum, Dr J. G. Baldacchino. Two outside experts, Professor Stuart Piggott of the University of Edinburgh, and Mr J. B. Ward Perkins, Director of the British School at Rome, were invited to visit Malta as Commissioners to assess the situation and advise the Committee on the best means of carrying out the work.

On their advice, new drawings and photographs of all the prehistoric pottery and other objects in the Museum were commissioned, to be made by members of the Museum staff, and new surveys of the field monuments, to be carried out by students of Architecture of the University of Malta. Finally, I was asked if I would undertake the task of supervising and co-ordinating these activities, and ultimately of writing the report.

The full results of the Prehistoric Survey of Malta will, it is hoped, shortly be published as an official record and corpus of material. The present volume is intended simply as a short account of the prehistoric cultures of Malta as they appear in the light of the new conclusions which I have been able to draw about their development, dating and relation with those of neighbouring lands, as a result of my work on the Survey during the past few years. These conclusions go far to clear up most of the major problems of Maltese prehistory and make it possible at last to give a fairly connected account of the development of the Maltese islands in prehistoric times.

By means of a careful study of the existing excavated material, followed by a series of small-scale excavations at carefully selected sites, it was possible to recognize, and establish on an objective basis, the existence of eight separate phases in the prehistoric occupation of the islands. Five of these illustrated the gradual development of the culture of the first people to colonize Malta (who to the end seem to have been without metal for tools and weapons), whilst the remaining three are constituted by the remains of people who came to Malta at a later date from Italy and Sicily (the first arrivals probably putting an end to the earlier culture), and who were technologically at a stage when they used tools of copper or bronze along with stone ones. The last of these phases was still in progress when men of Phoenician stock from Carthage came to make a base in the islands, which seems to have happened somewhere in the 8th century B.C. The fresh scrutiny of the prehistoric material further suggested many hitherto unsuspected contacts between the Maltese cultures and those of other Mediterranean lands, which have made it possible to assign approximate dates to each of the phases, based on the dating of the cultures with which they show contacts.

The bulk of the book is devoted to the remarkable culture elaborated by the people whose development fills the first five phases, the folk who built and equipped the great megalithic temples which are the most arresting monuments of antiquity in the Maltese islands. This is not simply because we know most about them, but because their remains are the testimony of a unique cultural achievement. In their remote islands, and in the service of their strange religion, these people produced architecture, sculpture, modelling and pottery whose aesthetic qualities we can still appreciate today. They did not do this entirely in isolation: one of the major results of the reexamination of the material has been to confirm the suggestion made long ago by Albert Mayr, Sir Arthur Evans and other archaeologists, that the masterpieces of Maltese art and architecture were produced under the stimulus of contact with the brilliant Minoan and Mycenean civilizations of Crete and Greece. Nevertheless, this scarcely detracts from the originality of the Maltese culture. Other nearby regions, such as parts of Italy and Sicily, were in even closer contact with the Aegean civilizations without producing anything comparable. In the Maltese islands the products of Eastern Mediterranean art and skill awoke the slumbering aesthetic sense of a naturally gifted people and resulted in products of a standard not again known in Western Europe until nearly a thousand years later.

It is for this reason that three full chapters have been devoted to them, and only one to the various groups of people who inhabited the islands in the later prehistoric period, but who produced no comparable achievements. Before we begin the examination of the remains of the Maltese templebuilders, however, it will be necessary to say a few words about the formation of the Maltese islands themselves and their earlier history up to the time when they were first occupied by man.

CHAPTER I

The Making of Malta

Fig. 1

Malta is the largest and most important of a compact group of islands which lies in the centre of the Mediterranean, about 60 miles from the south-east corner of Sicily. The others are Gozo, Comino, Cominotto and Filfla, but they are so rarely referred to in speaking of Malta, that many people think of it as a single, isolated island. Only one of these others, Gozo, is of importance to us, as it happens, since it is the only one apart from Malta which has any considerable remains of prehistoric times. This is not to be wondered at, since the rest are too small ever to have been of much significance. Comino, the largest, is just one mile in width and a little over a mile in length, and nothing earlier than a solitary grave of the Roman period has been found there. Cominotto and Filfla are just rocky islets, and are uninhabited at the present day, though a few sherds of prehistoric pottery have been collected from the latter. Comino (a name which means the cummin plant) and Cominotto lie in the strait between Malta and Gozo; Filfla, now used as a target for gunnery practice, is situated three miles off the south-west coast of Malta, and almost opposite the great prehistoric temples of Ħaġar Qim and Mnajdra.

Malta itself is 17·5 miles long and 8·3 miles wide, with an area of 93 sq. miles. Its longest axis is oriented north-west/south-east, and this line is continued north-westwards by the long axis of Gozo, which is 9 miles long and 4·5 miles wide, with an area of 26 sq. miles. The channel between the two is about 5 miles across. All the islands of the Maltese group are composed entirely of sedimentary, or water-laid rocks, a fact which seems at first surprising considering the number of active and extinct volcanoes in the vicinity. Apart from the very well known ones such as Etna and Vesuvius, there are a number of volcanic islands including Ischia, the Lipari Islands, and Stromboli (whose volcano was extinct, but made news recently by becoming active again). All of these lie to the north of Sicily, but to the south there is Linosa, only about 70 miles west of Malta, and the submarine Graham-volcano at a similar distance to the north-west. The vulcanicity of the region is, in fact, so striking that it probably gave rise to the oft-repeated story that some at least of the little flat-topped hills of Gozo mark the site of extinct volcanoes—a myth which is, needless to say, completely devoid of any other foundation.

The sedimentary deposits composing the Maltese islands were all laid down within a comparatively short period of geological time. They belong entirely to the Oligocene and Miocene periods of the Tertiary geological epoch. This means that, according to the estimates of geologists, their formation must have been taking place between about forty million and fifteen million years ago. There are, also, some localized traces of deposits of the succeeding, or Quaternary, geological epoch (the period of the Ice Age in Northern Europe), which began probably less than a million years ago. These are found chiefly in the valleys or on the sea coast, or as filling in fissures or caves. A large proportion of these Quaternary deposits must have been removed by subsequent denudation, leaving only the odd patches which we now find. During this period early forms of man had already appeared in some parts of the world, but we have no reliable evidence that any of them made their homes in the area which is now the Maltese islands.

The Tertiary rocks of Malta are mostly limestones, but there are also deposits of greensand and blue clay. The limestones are of great importance, since they provide the building stone which was used to erect the great prehistoric temples, and which is still the chief building material of the islands. The blue clay is also of great importance, since it is impervious to water, and the islands' water supply depends to some extent upon it, particularly in the West and North. All these deposits were laid down originally on an ancient sea bed. The waters which covered them varied in depth from time to time according to various geological changes affecting the coastline of the sea of which they formed part, and this in turn affected the nature of the deposits themselves.

Two main kinds of limestones can be found in Malta. These are the so-called Globigerina and Coralline limestones. The Globigerina limestone, composed almost entirely of minute fragments of the shells of molluscs, is soft, and of a deep yellow colour generally. It yields blocks of stone that can be pared into shape with the aid of a suitable implement, like lumps of cheese; but when exposed to the weather, they quickly develop a protective skin, or patina, on the surface which is quite resistant until it is broken at any point. Once this happens, however, the stone decays rapidly. It has been the main building stone in use since the Roman period at least.

The Coralline limestone, which varies in colour from nearly white to red, cream or grey, is much harder than the Globigerina, but less even in texture. It varies in composition, being often crystalline or semi-crystalline in structure. Some types will take a good polish, and are known as Gozo or Malta marbles. This stone was used extensively for building in its rough state in prehistoric times, on account of its hardness and resistance to weathering. The Globigerina, on the other hand, tended to be reserved for special purposes. The tendency of the Coralline limestone to fissure both horizontally and vertically, thus producing natural 'megalithic' slabs and boulders, no doubt helped to suggest the style of building with large stones which we find practised by the early inhabitants of the Maltese islands.

The stratigraphy of the rocks is the same in all the islands. At the top comes the Upper Coralline limestone, about

250 ft thick, but often considerably eroded; below that is the greensand layer, about 50 ft thick; next, 30 ft of blue clay, then the Globigerina limestone (about 200 ft of it), and finally the Lower Coralline limestone, which is known to be over 500 ft thick. What rocks are further down is not known; but this takes us down to sea/level, and what happens beneath is not of great interest to us here. The rocks of Malta are tilted downwards somewhat from south/west to north/east, so that the south/west coast is generally steep and abrupt, with cliffs that sometimes rise sheer out of the water for over 400 ft, whilst the north/east coast shelves gently into the sea. This tilting is continuing steadily at the present day, so that the north/east coast is gradually sinking below sea/level, whilst the cliffs of the south/west are crumbling slowly through weathering and falling into the sea.

I have already mentioned that the rocks of the Maltese islands were accumulated on the bed of a sea. This sea, which geologists call the Tethys, goes back to a very ancient period of the earth's history and covered a very much larger area than the present Mediterranean. In the latest period of the Tertiary epoch, the Pliocene, there was a regression of this sea, and the Maltese islands rose above its surface and became dry land. That is why there are no rocks of the Pliocene period in the islands. During this regression the sea fell well below its present level, and it seems certain that at some point the Maltese islands became joined to the land mass which comprised Sicily and South Italy, and that this situation continued until well into the Quaternary epoch. However, there has been much controversy as to whether they were also joined to the North African coast, and if so, when. The Maltese islands rise out of a relatively shallow bank which runs all the way from Sicily to the North African coast near Tunis, where the depth is never more than 200 fathoms (1200 ft). But the depth between Malta and Sicily is always less than 100 fathoms, and for most of the way less than 50 fathoms, so that it would be quite possible for the Maltese islands to be joined to Sicily without being at the same time joined to North Africa. The evidence seems definitely to support the idea that this was the case, at any rate during the Quaternary, or Pleistocene period. The French palaeontologist Vaufrey has demonstrated that the Pleistocene fauna of Malta, whose bones are found in the fissures and caves mentioned above as containing Quaternary deposits, is definitely related to the European rather than to the African fauna of the period. Against this, the Maltese botanist J. Borġ has claimed that the flora of Malta is of an African type only otherwise found in isolated outposts of Southern Europe, but Soos has shown that the Malaco-fauna and molluscs of present-day Malta are closely related to those of Sicily and contain no African elements. This suggests that if the Maltese islands were ever joined to North Africa, they were isolated from it again much sooner than from Sicily and Europe.

At some point during the Quaternary, however, the sea again cut off the islands from Sicily and they have remained isolated from them until the present day. This renewed isolation may be reflected in a curious way in some of the fauna. In fissures in the rock and in caves such as the Għar Dalam (Għar is Maltese for cave) have been found the bones of innumerable dwarf elephants and hippopotami. Three species of elephants have been distinguished according to size, the smallest being only 3 ft high when fully grown. They are all related to *Elephas antiquus,* the European elephant of the Pleistocene period. Similar, though not identical, dwarf elephants have been found in deposits in other islands of the Mediterranean, such as Sicily, Sardinia, Crete and Cyprus. In some stratified sites it can be demonstrated that the smaller ones are later than the larger ones, because they are found higher up in the deposits. A plausible explanation of this is that a number of beasts of normal size were trapped on the newly formed islands and that

Fig. 1 (1)
Plate 1

35

their descendants decreased in size owing to a scarcity of fodder and worsening conditions generally. This hypothesis also has the merit of explaining why species of dwarf animals found on different islands are not identical, since they would have developed in isolation from each other, though along roughly parallel lines.

At Ghar Dalam the layer above that in which the hippos and elephants were found contains chiefly the bones of red deer, so that either the Sicilian connection must have been renewed again for a short time, or else it was not actually broken until after the period of the deer. In 1917 great excitement was caused by the finding, allegedly in this level, mixed with the bones of deer, of two human teeth of a curious type. They are molars, but the roots, instead of being separate, as in normal human teeth, are fused together. This is a phenomenon known technically as *taurodontism,* and it is particularly characteristic of the primitive type of human known as Neanderthal man. Sir Arthur Keith, to whom they were submitted, admitted them as sufficient evidence for the presence of this primitive kind of man in the Maltese islands. Unfortunately no other remains of Neanderthal man have been found at Ghar Dalam or elsewhere in the islands, and recently Dr J. G. Baldacchino has discovered the presence of taurodontism in the teeth from some of the skulls of people buried in the Hal Saflieni Hypogeum—skulls belonging to a much later period and of normal Homo Sapiens type! It seems most likely that the two Ghar Dalam teeth come from one of the burials in the upper layers (of which a number are recorded), and worked their way down, or were carried by worms, into the level where they were found. Thus there are as yet no trustworthy traces of the presence of man in Malta before the Neolithic period.

Because of their central position in the Mediterranean, the tiny Maltese islands have been of immense strategic and commercial importance throughout most of their long and

chequered history. Often enough, from the palmy days of
Carthage onwards, they have been the jealously guarded
possession of a great sea power, or the appanage of a great
empire. It was not, however, for this reason that the first colony
of Neolithic farmers came to Malta. They came across the
strait from Sicily in their primitive boats simply in search of a
new home and more land to cultivate. In these early days
farming meant continual movement and expansion of peoples
as families grew and land lost its fertility through cultivation,
since the use of manures and rotation of crops were still
unknown. It seems likely, too, that at that time the Maltese
islands were more fertile and attractive than at present, with a
more abundant vegetation (as the tusks of wild boars and
antler of deer found in the early deposits seem to indicate),
which would help to retain the light soil and prevent the rain-
water from running straight off into the sea. Thus two of Malta's
main problems today—soil erosion and the loss of rain-water—
were probably considerably less acute then. The Maltese islands
as they then were must have provided a nearly perfect setting for
a peaceful and industrious people to develop a material culture
and civilization all their own. The remains which have come
down to us from this time show that the early Maltese took full
advantage of their opportunities, for their temples, carving
and sculpture, as well as other objects, are of a quality unique
in Western Europe in prehistoric times.

Despite its powerfully individual expression, however, this
culture has also something of the character of a solitary outpost
of Near Eastern and Aegean civilization in the barbarian West.
For the importance of Malta as a key to the trade of the
Western Mediterranean was not long in being discovered.
There is some evidence that quite early in the second millennium B.C. ships from the Aegean islands of the Cyclades may
have called there, and it seems certain that a little later, about
the middle of that millennium, the trade-goods of the powerful

Minoan and Mycenean civilizations of Crete and Greece exercised a profound effect on the development of the various arts in Malta. Perhaps the Mycenean merchants made a base in Malta for the purposes of trade with the lands further west, as they certainly did in the Lipari islands. Unfortunately we have as yet no direct evidence for this in Malta such as Dr Bernabò Brea has found in Lipari, in the shape of actual Mycenean pottery, and so we have to argue from the indirect evidence of the influences that appear in the works of native Maltese craftsmen. These are so obvious, however, that we may hope that some day more direct evidence will be forthcoming.

It will be seen from the foregoing that, though there are still gaps in the evidence, it is possible to say quite a lot about these earliest inhabitants of Malta, their culture and their customs. The purpose of the following chapter is to set out this knowledge in greater detail.

CHAPTER II

The Earliest Maltese

M AN REACHED the Maltese islands relatively late.
Throughout the long period of the Old Stone Age
there is, as we have seen, nothing to indicate that any of the
early hunters pursued their game into that small corner of what
was then a great land mass which included both Sicily and
Italy, and reached out towards the coast of North Africa.
Abundant remains of the activities of such hunting bands have
been found in various parts of Sicily, however, where some of
the caves which they inhabited lie within a hundred miles of
Malta. The two human teeth, already mentioned in the last
chapter, were once thought to provide evidence that at any
rate a few individuals of the primitive Neanderthal type had
once lived in the Għar Dalam, but since it has been shown that
these do not necessarily belong to Neanderthalers, it seems that
once more we have no reason to suppose that Palaeolithic man
ever set foot on the ground which now forms the islands of the
Maltese group. Once they had become divided from Sicily by
the sea, the tiny islands could have had little attraction for
hunting societies, even if these had had the means of crossing
the sea to reach them, which in itself is doubtful. At all events,
it seems almost certain that they did not do so; the islands
reserved their charms for later people with a quite different way
of life.

For many thousands of years the miniature archipelago,
though at that time the main islands were probably well-
wooded, fertile and abounding in game, lay uninhabited,
awaiting the advent of men who would at last recognize in
it a desirable home for the taking. Meanwhile the rigours of
the last Ice Age were passing away from Europe; with the
changing climatic conditions the fauna changed also to a more

or less modern type, and corresponding adjustments took place in the hunting societies which subsisted chiefly on the fauna. By and large they adapted themselves relatively successfully to the new conditions, though on the whole population seems to have become sparser in Southern Europe, for the great days of the hunting societies were already over in our continent.

The developments just mentioned found no echo in the uninhabited islands off the south-east coast of Sicily, though of course the climatic changes must have made some difference. But other developments were taking place elsewhere which were to be crucial for their history. Far away in the East, revolutionary changes were coming about in the way of life of some human groups, which were discovering how to produce their own food instead of relying on hunting and gathering. The domestication of plants and animals led to a more stable and settled existence than that which had hitherto been possible, and gradually proved to have opened up hitherto undreamed-of possibilities for the development and enrichment of human culture. With the immediate triumphs of civilization to which these discoveries were soon to lead in the regions of the Near East where they were first made, we are not concerned; they are of importance to us rather because they were the remote cause of the Maltese islands ceasing to be an uninhabited paradise for wild animals, and becoming, if not a paradise, at least a favourable and sheltered home for a remarkable human society.

Just as a stone dropped into water produces an ever-widening series of ripples, so the introduction of the new techniques of food-production in the Near East soon had repercussions over ever-expanding areas. How far this was due to movements of farmers in search of new land to cultivate, and how far to the adoption of the new methods by hunting peoples from neighbouring farmers is often doubtful, though it is certain that both these processes played a part. At all events, human groups practising a primitive kind of farming soon begin to appear in the archaeological record further and further away from the original centres. Along both the European and African coasts of the Mediterranean traces have been found of these earliest farming communities, who bred sheep, cattle and pigs and cultivated wheat and barley. Prominent among the remains left by these peoples are fragments of pottery, a product which came into general use only when settled life had made its weight and fragility less serious drawbacks than they had been for mobile hunting cultures. To the archaeologist these poor potsherds are more precious than gold for the light they can shed, properly interpreted, on the movements and interrelations of prehistoric human groups.

Many of the early Mediterranean farming communities used a kind of primitive pottery decorated with patterns which were impressed into the surface of the clay before the pot was baked, and which is for this reason known to archaeologists as 'impressed ware'. Pottery of this type has been found on the south-east coast of Turkey, in Greece, Italy, Sicily, Mediterranean France, Spain and the North African coast. Always this pottery is found in levels belonging to the earliest communities with a knowledge of farming in any given region, and it is fragments of this 'impressed pottery' which constitute the earliest remains of human activity so far identifiable in the Maltese islands.

Very little of this early pottery has been found in Malta, and by far the greatest number of sherds come from a single site, the Dalam cave, already often mentioned, from the deeper levels of which came the bones of the deer, dwarf elephants and hippopotami of an earlier day. The impressed pottery was stratified above the levels with animal bones, but unfortunately the upper levels in which it lay had been disturbed many times by later human activities in the cave, so that it was mixed with the remains of much later periods, down to Roman times and even later. Thus we can learn little more from this deposit

Fig. 1 (1)

Absolute Dates	Period	Phase	Type site	Pottery Decoration
	I	A	GHAR DALAM	Impressed
		B	MGARR	Broad cut-out bands
		C	ZEBBUG	Narrow cut-out bands
		D	GGANTIJA	Scratched
1600 B.C. 1500		E	TARXIEN	Scratched; applied; rusticated; studded; jabbed
1400	II	A	TARXIEN CEMETERY	Scored; shark's tooth; applied knobs
1300 1200		B	BORG IN-NADUR	Deep incision; studs
1100–800		C	BAHRIJA	Deep incision; excision

Table showing the development of the prehistoric cultures of the Maltese Islands, and their relation to the culture-sequer

Monuments	Contemporary Cultures in: S.E. Sicily	Lipari
None	Stentinello	Castellaro Vecchio
Simple rock-tombs; kidney-shaped building at Mġarr	Stentinello	Capri/Serra d'Alto
Rock-tombs; trefoil temple at Mġarr	San Cono	Diana
Rock-tombs; trefoil temples; first temples with two sets of chambers	Serraferlicchio/ S. Ippolito	Piano Conte/ Piano Quartara
Rock-tombs; hypogeum; temples with two and three sets of chambers	S. Ippolito Castelluccio	Capo Graziano
Cremation cemetery; dolmens'; etc.	Castelluccio	Capo Graziano
Fortified villages	Thapsos	Milazzese
Fortified village	Pantalica	Ausonian

Sicily and the Lipari Islands. The double lines indicate the arrival of new people from abroad than that people using impressed pottery were once living in Malta.

The potsherds from Għar Dalam are greyish or brownish in colour, and divide themselves roughly into two classes, those that are fragments of thick-walled, coarsely-made storage jars, and those that belong to smaller fine wares with thinner walls. The decoration also varies in complexity and in the care with which it is applied. Here again, though the gradations are more subtle than in the actual fabric, the more complex and carefully executed decoration tends to be found on the smaller, finer pots, and the cruder on the large coarse ones. The simplest decoration was a series of jabs made with a stick, sometimes arranged in rows, sometimes not. The more complex patterns were formed of lines drawn in the clay with the same instrument. The sherds are all too small to give much idea of what the general arrange-ment and effect of these patterns would have been, but so far as can be seen they were composed entirely of rectilinear geometric motifs. The most elaborate of these seems to have consisted of a plain zig-zag band formed by two interlocked rows of hatched triangles. Another sherd shows what seems to be part of a hatched chevron pattern. A further common pattern was made by blocks of parallel lines set at different angles, and sometimes separated by a plain band. These lines were often made with a shell edge instead of a stick, which gives them the appearance of small zig-zag lines. A number of these lines made with the edge of a *Cardium* shell and set close together produces an effect which a French archaeologist has called the 'velouté' or velvety appearance.

Because of the small quantity of material found, and the unfortunate circumstance of the upper levels at Għar Dalam being disturbed, we know very little about these first colonizers of the Maltese islands. It is, however, possible to infer a certain amount. In the first place, they must have reached their new home by sea. The nearest land is Sicily, separated from Malta

Plates 34, 35

Plate 34a, b, d, e

Plate 34c

Plate 35

Plate 35b
Plate 35a

Plate 35a, b

by a strait about 60 miles wide, and it was from Sicily that the people who colonized Malta came. We can say this with confidence, because the impressed pottery found in Malta is almost identical with that made and used by the earliest agricultural communities of Sicily, which has there been called the Stentinello type, after the name of the site where it was first found. Impressed pottery has many local varieties and the Sicilian variety is characterized by an exceptionally elaborate decoration, and so is easily recognizable. At one time it was thought that the first inhabitants of Malta might have come there from Africa, but, apart from the fact that the coast of North Africa is much further away than Sicily, the impressed pottery of Malta shows no especially close relationship with the varieties that have been found on sites in the adjoining parts of North Africa.

The colonization of the Maltese islands from Sicily was certainly not accidental, indeed it was logical and inevitable once that island was populated by more or less settled groups of farmers. From Cape Passero, at the south-eastern corner of the triangular island of Sicily, Malta and Gozo can be discerned on a clear day lying far out to sea. The land-hungry peasants who first crossed the straits to them knew exactly what they were about, and must have planned their expedition thoroughly. As well as themselves and their families, they had to transport their domestic animals and supplies of seed for cultivation. For this they must obviously have had boats of some kind, though not necessarily more elaborate than some form of raft or dug-out canoe. We know nothing more about their boats, however, than inference will tell us, since no remains of such boats or pictures of them have been found, and pictures of more or less contemporary East Mediterranean craft, such as have been found scratched on potsherds in Greece and the Cyclades, are no help, since the boats of the more primitive peoples of the Western Mediterranean were probably much cruder and simpler.

The Stentinello culture of Sicily almost certainly lasted for a long time—several hundred years at least—though it has not yet been possible to subdivide this period chronologically, since no stratified deposits of the period have yet been excavated. At what point during this period the colonizers of Malta left Sicily for their new home it is therefore as yet very difficult for us to say. It seems probable, though, that it was early on, since some of the more elaborate techniques used in decorating the Stentinello pottery, which are probably a late development, do not occur on the Maltese wares. One of these techniques, a very characteristic one, which is absent in Malta, is the use of patterned stamps for impressing the designs into the clay.

Plate 35a

Another, hardly found on the pottery of this first phase in Malta, though, as we shall see, it becomes important later, is that of cutting out broad shallow bands in the surface of the clay. With only such vague hints to indicate when the first colonizers left Sicily, it is obviously almost impossible at present to arrive at anything like an accurate date for this event in terms of years. However, since most authorities would be inclined to date the arrival of the first impressed-ware people in Sicily at about 3000 B.C., we shall probably not be too far wrong if we think of the first crossing to Malta as being made somewhere about the middle of the third millennium B.C.

The colonists, when they arrived in Malta, were in what archaeologists term a Neolithic stage of culture; that is, they knew the techniques of food production, they made pottery and polished as well as chipped stone implements, but they had no knowledge of the use of metals. The Maltese islands offer no resources for the development of metallurgy, and evidently these earliest Maltese got on quite happily without metal tools or adornments, since the remarkable culture which they founded remained without metal right to the end of its long development, though the nearby cultures of Sicily had by then been using copper and bronze for a considerable time.

This fact is of great importance, as well as being curious in itself, since it has misled some archaeologists in the past into dating the great megalithic temples that are the characteristic monument of the later phases of this culture much too early, simply because their builders used no metal tools. In fact, of course, such technological criteria have not necessarily any bearing on dates at all.

Apart from the sherds of impressed pottery, the only relics which we can recognize as definitely belonging to these earliest inhabitants are two small clay models representing heads of domesticated animals, sheep or cattle (they are so schematized that it is difficult to say which). These also come from the Dalam Cave, and we can safely associate them with the impressed pottery, because they are made of identical paste and decorated with jabs of a stick in the same way as the impressed pots. One at least was part of the rather elaborate handle of a pot. These figurines are extremely interesting and important for a number of reasons. First of all they confirm the interest of the colonizers in stock-breeding, and show that they brought over flocks and herds with them, and secondly they very closely resemble animal-head figurines found among remains of the Stentinello culture on Sicilian sites. Dr Bernabò Brea, the greatest expert on Sicilian archaeology, believes that the making of animal figurines of this type was not originally a habit of the Stentinello people, but that they adopted the idea from other people, who knew how to decorate their pottery with painted patterns, and who arrived in Italy and Sicily somewhat later than the 'impressed-ware' people. If this is so, it confirms that the Maltese impressed-ware people probably arrived relatively late, in all likelihood not before about 2500 B.C.

Plate 72

Once settled in the Maltese islands, the colonists began to go their own way, and soon were in process of developing a culture with many special features of its own, and only a general resemblance to those in the areas whence they originally came.

From now on we have better evidence for their activities, and we can follow this process quite closely, not only in the pottery, but also in the development of the special types of monument in which most of it has been found. These monuments are so-called megalithic temples and rock-cut tombs. We shall be dealing in detail with the development of these two forms of architecture in the next chapter, so that only general references to the course of their evolution will be made here. The development of the pottery, however, we shall follow more fully, since it is the most sensitive criterion of the changes that occurred. It is the sequence of stages which can be seen in the evolution of the pottery used by the early Maltese civilization that actually enables us to prove the direction taken in the architectural developments, besides giving us many hints as to Malta's relations with the outside world during this long period of time.

Figs. 2, 4a

The next stage, phase B, in the development of the Maltese culture to be discerned from the archaeological record shows it already with a marked individuality, if not yet rising to any remarkable height of achievement. Technically, the pottery of this second phase shows strong continuity with the impressed pottery of the first phase, though it is generally better fired and is usually highly polished. Most of the pieces are dark grey or black in colour, though a few have a yellowish surface. The decoration, however, shows an almost complete break-away from that favoured earlier. Instead of being impressed in the clay of the pot before firing, it was now made by cutting out broad, shallow bands of clay from the surface of the pot, which were afterwards filled with a white paste up to the original level of the surface. This was done to make the pattern stand out. The actual cutting out was probably done with a sharp flint knife of which many have been found on the sites, and could have been done either before or after the pot was fired. Often a series of short shallow lines were scratched diagonally across the edges of their grooves. Whether this was to help the adherence of the paste or for decorative effect, or even to reproduce in some measure the effect of the irregular edge of blocks of lines done with a *Cardium* shell it is difficult to say.

The change in the patterns themselves is no less remarkable than the change in the methods of applying them. Rectilinear

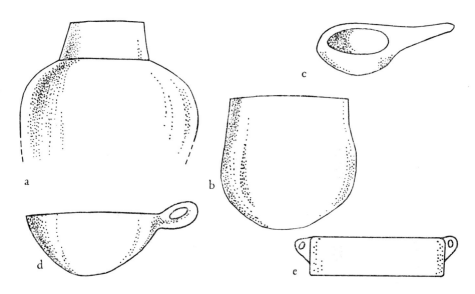

Fig. 2   Pottery shapes of phase IB. Not to scale

patterns like those of the previous phase have become rare, their place being taken by patterns made up chiefly of curved lines. Once again it is difficult to get an idea of the general effect of these patterns because of the fragmentary state of most of the pottery belonging to this phase, though things are not quite so bad as they are for the previous phase, since there are very many more pieces to study, some of which are quite large; there are even one or two more or less complete pots. The large

Fig 2b, a

Fig. 2e
Fig. 2c, d

Fig. 4a

pieces and complete pots enable us to get some idea of the range of shapes made, which seems to be rather restricted. By far the most common are simple bowls and jars, the latter sometimes having a more or less conical neck separated from the body. It is probable that these jars had cylindrical clay covers with two or four horizontal lug-handles around the top. A few clay spoons and little cups fitted with a single loop handle which rises well above the rim also seem likely to date from this phase, though it is difficult to be sure, since they come from old excavations and their exact context is not recorded.

The bowls and neckless jars generally have from one to three horizontal cut-out bands just below the rim. From these, other bands, sometimes single, but more usually in batches of two or more, fall away vertically or diagonally. These divide the field of the vase into panels, across which batches of parallel grooves swing round in graceful curves to join them. Sometimes, however, the grooves that cross the panels do not run parallel, but close together towards one end. These are the first examples of a motif, the so-called 'comet' pattern, which was elaborately developed in pottery decoration in a later phase.

Apart from those on the small cups, true handles are not used as yet. When the pots are fitted with handles they are of the string-hole variety, or else unpierced knobs of clay. A very curious form of handle is a small tubular lug set vertically just below the rim of a pot. At the top of this a hole is drilled vertically to a small depth, whilst at the bottom another is pierced horizontally into the wall of the vase, though not so as to go right through it. How this was actually used is uncertain, but it is possible that the ends of suitably bent sticks were inserted into the holes of a pair of these 'partly-pierced' lugs on opposite sides of a vase for the purpose of lifting it off a fire when hot. The decoration runs over the lugs quite often, as it did also in the previous phase, and it is often especially elaborate around the 'partly-pierced' lugs.

The pottery that has just been described has been found in rock-cut tombs and on the sites of megalithic temples. Most of the large temple-complexes excavated in Malta and Gozo have yielded some examples of it, but by far the greatest quantities come from relatively small and primitive complexes, where little had taken place in the way of later reconstruction. The most important of these temple-sites is the one which lies on the edges of the village of Mġarr, on the south-west coast of Malta. This consists of two buildings, both relatively simple in plan, but one is smaller and more primitive in construction than the other. Excavations made here in 1954 proved that the smaller building dated from this second phase. A trench cut down to bed rock in this building revealed that the floors of the building had been renewed several times, the later ones being made of *torba* (a kind of cement made of crushed lime-stone), the earlier ones simply of beaten earth. Beneath each of these floors potsherds and other debris were found. Below the lowest floor all the sherds found had decoration of the cut-out type, whilst in the levels above this sherds with later types of decoration occurred. The stratigraphy found in this trench was, incidentally, the first actual proof that the pottery sequence as worked out by study of the materials in the Museum was correct.

A part from the material from Mġarr, the greatest quantity of sherds with cut-out decoration has come from a series of very ruined structures on Kordin Hill, above the Grand Harbour. Most of these rather primitive buildings were excavated long ago, and one or two were destroyed by enemy action during the Second World War. The most important, however, a complex called Kordin III, which included some larger and better preserved buildings than the others, survived undamaged; here in 1954 it was possible to obtain another stratigraphy, consisting this time of several superimposed floors of beaten earth, and it confirmed the one at Mġarr. This stratigraphy was

Fig. 1 (2)
Plate 2

Fig. 13 (1)

found outside the area of relatively well-preserved buildings, which were shown to date from a later phase; it was unfortunately not possible therefore to relate it to any surviving building. This was due partly to the very wrecked condition of the building remains in the area, partly to the fact that most of the deposit had been dug away in the original excavations of Peet and Ashby in 1909.

Fig. 1 (27)
Figs. 14, 15
Plates 32, 33

Pottery of the cut-out type was also found in some of the rock-cut tombs excavated in 1955 on the Xemxija Heights above the western side of St Paul's Bay on the north coast of Malta. In this case only a few sherds were found, but they are sufficient to show that at any rate some of these tombs were in use already in this phase. A fair quantity of this same pottery is among the material recovered in the excavations made before the First World War in the great labyrinth of rock-cut chambers known as the Hal Saflieni Hypogeum. Though no direct information is available as to exactly where these were found in the building, it is possible to deduce from the fact that pottery of this type is not mentioned in the report on the pottery published in 1910 by Tagliaferro, that it must have come from the part nearest the entrance, which was not excavated until 1911–12. This part of the structure must be the earliest, and the workmanship of these chambers is in fact much rougher than that which went to the making of the inner halls.

Thus we know from finds of the cut-out pottery in each that by this time the prototypes of both the megalithic and rock-cut buildings, whose architecture was to be so marvellously developed later, were being built by the inhabitants of the Maltese islands. Though we cannot assign any of these structures to the first phase, the continuity of this culture with that of the first colonists is shown by the occasional occurrence of sherds of impressed pottery on temple-sites. Three come from Mġarr, and a small handful from the Gozitan sites of Santa Verna and Xewkija. About the rest of the material culture of the

Maltese of this second phase we can still say very little. A small dumb-bell-shaped hammer of stone and a fossil shark's tooth were found with the pottery in the trench at Mġarr, but apart from that all is guesswork. On analogies with Sicily we might assign some of the large, roughly made flint blades and scrapers

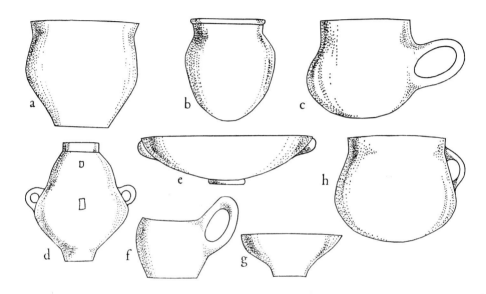

Fig. 3 Pottery shapes of phase IC. Not to scale

found at Mġarr and Kordin to this phase, and it is probable that they also used bone awls, as was done in later phases, and was common practice among Neolithic cultures.

As was mentioned earlier, the cut-out techniques of decoration were also used on the Stentinello pottery of Sicily. It occurs also once alongside the impressed technique on a sherd from the Għar Dalam in Malta. Both these facts serve to emphasize the continuity of the pottery—and therefore of the general cultural and ethnic—tradition between the two phases in the Maltese islands. In days before pottery became an in-dustrial product, when it was home-made, generally by the women of the community for local use, such an assumption is a fairly safe one. An internal development with little interference from the outside world is also indicated by the fact that apart from general analogies in the technique of pottery decoration and perhaps flint working, there is now little to connect the Maltese culture with Sicily, or indeed with any neighbouring country. The curvilinear patterns of the Maltese wares are not found on the Stentinello pottery. There is no trace either in Sicily of stone structures like the early Maltese temples, nor are there any parallels to the rock-cut tombs, though indeed little is known of the burial practices of the Stentinello people, for hardly any of their tombs have been found. Most of the Stenti-nello sites are either in caves or settlements in the open, which are sometimes surrounded with rock-cut ditches. Conversely, no settlement sites of any kind have yet been found in Malta belonging to this first civilization, so that no comparisons can be made.

The picture we get from the remains of the second phase of a local culture beginning to develop its own idiosyncrasies and way of life in comparative isolation is confirmed in a general way by the material which survives from the next distinguishable phase (C). Once again pottery must be our chief criterion, and we are fortunate now in having much larger quantities to study, including a whole series of complete vases. Technically, this pottery of the third phase shows very clearly its descent from the wares of the preceding phase, though a number of innovations are also found. The most common ware is identical in firing and finishing with that of the second phase. The surface is polished and grey or black in colour. But a second type of ware is now also present, with a surface of a striking light-yellow colour. The surface of this ware, though sometimes polished, is more often left matt, and the paste of which it is made is

Plates 36–38
Figs. 3–6

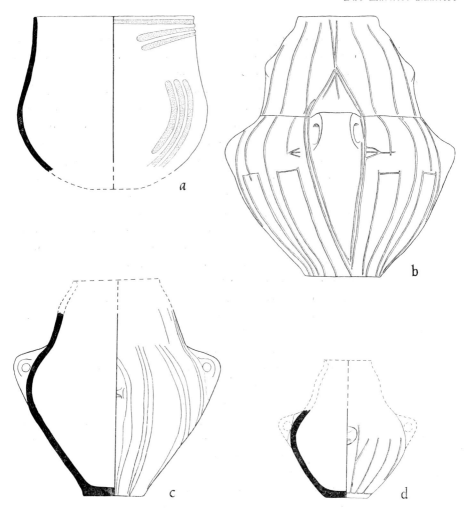

Fig. 4 Pottery of phase IC. a, c, d, from tomb 1 at Zebbuġ; b from Baldacchino Collection, provenance unknown. Height of g 10 in., others to scale

coarser than that of the dark polished wares, frequently containing small stones, and seems to be less well-fired. This ware
is in one sense a development of the yellow-faced pieces of the

preceding phase, but its popularity in this period may also be due to influences from the cultures in Italy and Sicily which used painted pottery, since this invariably had a yellow or buff surface, whereon the paint was laid.

The decoration which is used equally on both these types of ware is a development of that used in the second phase. It is once more made by cutting out the clay with a flint knife, but this time the bands are much narrower, so much so that they now usually have a V-shaped section instead of being more or less flat at the bottom. The incised fringes are succeeded by rows of tiny cut-out triangles or lines of dots bordering the grooves. Some sherds might fairly be described as transitional, for instance those whereon the few broad cut-out bands have been replaced by a larger number of narrow grooves bordered by dots, forming elongated isosceles triangles which hang down from the rim of the vessel.

The usual decoration, however, is now based generally on pairs of parallel lines, or sometimes on batches of four at a time. Sometimes also the single line occurs, often not straight, but wavy or zig-zag. The patterns are partly rectilinear, partly curvilinear. Generally there is a mixture of both, but on any one vase one or other generally predominates sufficiently to provide the keynote of the whole. The favourite curvilinear motif is a semicircular or ogival pattern arranged in panels outlined by vertical and horizontal lines. One of the most curious and distinctive features of this style is the practice of incising one or more irregular lines inside the mouths of vases just below the rim (which is often milled, as it was also in the preceding phase). Even more interesting, however, is the tendency to introduce schematized human figures. Two examples are known possessing triangular heads, stick-like arms and legs, and no body at all to speak of. More common, however, are ambiguous, vaguely anthropomorphic shapes made by drawing rough 'ghost'-like bodies with stick-like

Fig. 5a, c
Fig. 5b

Plate 36
Fig. 5c

Fig. 5c
Fig. 6a

Plate 37

arms and generally three-fingered hands around perforated
lugs, which presumably suggested a pair of eyes to the makers
of the vases. Vertical lines are often broken up by a curious

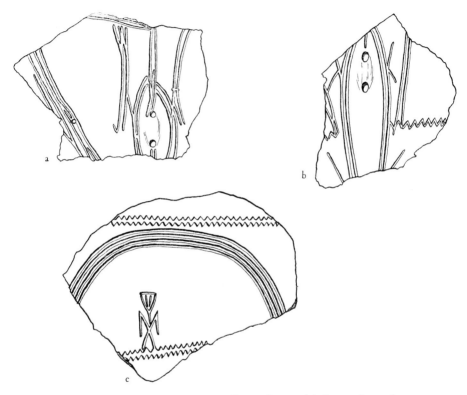

*Fig. 5   Fragments of decorated pottery from the Zebbuġ tombs; a and b from tomb 5, c from
tomb 4. Breadth of c $5\frac{1}{16}$ in., others to scale*

'crossed flail' motif, giving them a sort of 'corn-stalk' appearance,
but whether this was also intended to suggest the human form
it would be difficult to say. We are here in a world of primitive
symbols, whose significance—which may have been great to
their originators—must in all probability escape us for ever.

Plate 38

57

Plate 37
Fig. 4*b*–*d*

Such complete vases as survive give us a pretty good idea of the main types of vessel in use in this period. The most characteristic and distinctive shape is a jar with a curious bell-shaped neck set on a pear-shaped body which rests on a small flat base. This is the first occurrence of the flat base in Maltese pottery. There are also simplified versions of this jar, where the neck loses its bell-shape, becoming more like an inverted cone with slightly concave sides. These vases are equipped with stout horizontal lug-handles set opposite each other on the shoulder, and from two to four lesser lugs or decorative knobs at right angles to them on the neck or shoulder. The finest examples are rather dignified and impressive, if somewhat strange, vases. Hole-mouth jars and full-bodied jars with squat conical or cylindrical necks are only known from sherds. Other common shapes are an ovoid jar or bowl with wide mouth and heavy rolled rim, hemispherical bowls, shallow bowls with unpierced or 'partly-pierced' lugs set on the rim, and deep bag-shaped bowls, generally with a thin broad strap-handle. Cups with an oval strap-handle or a horizontally-pierced lug on the lower part of the body also occur, as well as open bowls with a flat base, sometimes simple, rarely in the form of a pedestal. Rarer forms are a bell-shaped jar and a rough, high-handled cup.

Fig. 3*b*

Fig. 3*b*
Fig. 3*c*

Fig. 3*e*
Plate 38
Fig. 3*f*

The bell-necked jars are invariably decorated with one of two relatively stereotyped schemes, one of which is predominantly curvilinear and the other predominantly rectilinear in its total effect. In the former the field is quartered vertically by means of groups of two or three vertical lines, and divided horizontally by a line which marks the separation of neck and shoulder. The panels thus formed are filled with ogival patterns, as described above. In the lower panels, which are the larger, two interlocking semicircles are surmounted by a third. The rectilinear type has the field quartered in the same way, except that in this case the lines break up to surround the lugs. Neck

Plate 37
Fig. 4*b*

and body are again divided. The neck is decorated with a series of verticals between the quarterings, whilst each of the lower panels is filled with three vertical lines, of which the two outer ones cease about a third of the way down, where they meet the bases of two inverted isosceles triangles. There are further minor variants of each of these two types.

As can be seen from the catalogue of shapes, all the types of lug which are found on the pottery of the second phase are still used during this one, but in addition there are now true handles

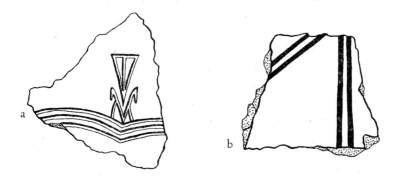

Fig. 6 Fragments of decorated pottery from the Zebbuġ tombs; a from tomb 4, b from tomb 5. Breadth of a 2 in., other to scale

of the 'strap' variety. Some of the cups and bowls having these handles are very thin-walled and light, as are the handles themselves, and constitute quite a *tour de force* of primitive potting.

Apart from the normal pottery just discussed, there are also a number of fragments decorated with painted patterns which belong to this phase. Almost all of these are of a yellow or ivory colour and painted in red or brown, but there are a few frag-ments of dark-faced ware which are decorated with broad bands of a thin, greyish-white paint. The latter may belong to the end of the preceding phase, whose pottery they resemble in

Fig. 6b

general effect, but the light-coloured wares are firmly connected with the third phase. The ware itself is very similar to, often identical with, the light incised wares of this phase. The patterns are often identical also with those on the yellow-faced incised wares, which, it may be noted, had their incised patterns filled with red instead of white paste, so that the general effect must have been closely similar to that of the painted wares. The painted pottery is only known from mostly quite small fragments, but these are sometimes large enough to show the shape of the vase from which they come; when this is the case the shape is always one known in the incised-ware repertoire of the phase. Finally, four fragments of the painted ware were found, along with incised ware belonging to the third phase, in one of a group of tombs of this period found near the village of Zebbuġ.

The pottery we have been discussing is again found on most of the main sites in Malta and Gozo, but the most important *Fig. 1 (6)* for the study of this phase are the Mġarr temples and a group *Fig. 16* of five rock-cut tombs just mentioned which were found during building operations near Zebbuġ. At Mġarr, the larger *Fig. 13 (2)* of the two temples was shown by the pottery found at the bottom of a trial trench to have been built in this phase, though, like the smaller monument it continued in use to the very end of the civilization of the Maltese temple-builders. It is constructed of larger stones than the earlier temple, and shows considerable architectural advance, though the basic plan is still simple. The most striking innovation is the provision of a monumental façade; this is concave and encloses a semicircular forecourt. The introduction of this feature might perhaps, as we shall see, be due to foreign influence from some culture with which the Maltese were in contact at this time.

The tombs are really of the greatest interest. They are, as previously stated, five in number, and when found were simply shallow oval depressions in the rock, though it seems most likely that they were originally small rock-cut chamber tombs. The soft limestone of Malta has been so often cut and quarried away that there is no improbability in this; indeed, there are

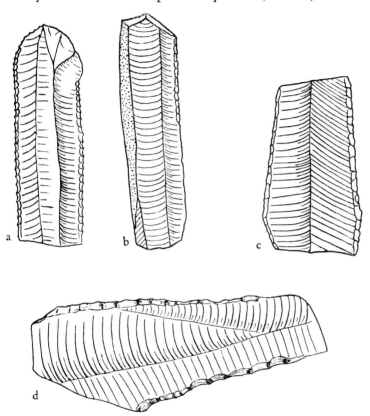

Fig. 7   Flint blades from the Zebbuġ tombs, a from tomb 5, b and d from tomb 4, c from tomb 1. Length of a 1½ in., others to scale

several other examples of the same thing. However, the deposit on the floor of the tombs had been left intact, and provided a rich haul of material all dating from this phase. Apart from the small amounts of material recovered from the trial trenches at Mġarr and Kordin, sealed in below floors, this is the earliest closed find we have in Malta, and it for the first time enables us to get a slightly more complete picture of the material culture of the early Maltese. The little group of tombs must have been used only over a very short period, which is unusual in Malta, though very fortunate for us.

Apart from the human bones and the bones of animals probably put in as offerings, the material from the Zebbuġ tombs

Figs. 8, 7

consists only of a few shell beads and buttons, four flint blades and one or two objects of softer stone. Three types of shell were used. The small, tube⁄like *Dentalium* shells were threaded as they were, and *Pectunculus* shells simply pierced for suspension, but pieces of *Spondylus* shell were cut to form beads and buttons.

Fig. 8a–c
Fig. 8e

There are several barrel⁄shaped beads of this shell, and a small domical button with a V⁄shaped thread⁄hole on its flat side, a type of button which is found in many other areas, especially in the Western Mediterranean, and which is therefore of great importance as evidence for the foreign contacts and relative date of this phase in Malta. The flint blades are small, 3 to 4 cm.

Fig. 7

long, and have been retouched with great care along the cutting edges, but are otherwise quite unremarkable. Of the two objects of softer stone, one is a kind of limestone mortar or basin, the other a very important find, of which we shall have to say more later. It is the earliest dateable piece of sculpture in the

Plate 48

Maltese islands, consisting of a flat slab of globigerina lime⁄stone carved with a very rough and schematized representation of a human face on one side. The slab is broken off at the bottom, but the beginnings of a shoulder are discernible, showing that the figure had originally a body as well. This

Fig. 16

object was found lying among the remains in tomb 5.

The culture of the third phase is emphatically Maltese in all respects. It is the product of an already quite long gestation in its homeland, and is a unique phenomenon, not only as regards its material, but also its psychological side. The religious hypertrophy which was to become so startlingly marked in the latest phases is already well advanced. The disposal of the dead, temple building and the cults associated with it are already, one feels, absorbing all the surplus energies of the islanders. Nevertheless, though developed in comparative isolation, this culture grew from a stock originally transplanted from elsewhere, and there is good evidence that it maintained contacts of a fairly regular kind with the outer world throughout the whole process. The Maltese islands are deficient in many resources highly necessary to a primitive society, and these could only be supplied by trade carried on across the sea, not only with

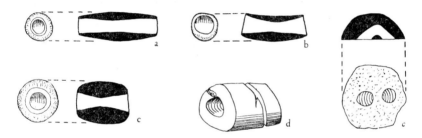

Fig. 8 Shell (a–c, e) and bone (d) beads from the Zebbuġ tombs, a–c from tomb 4, d, e tomb 5 Diameter of e ¾ in., others to scale

the people of Sicily, and southern Italy, but probably also, directly or indirectly, with countries even further afield.

Contacts with Sicily are abundantly confirmed by the ceramic evidence. The style of the Zebbuġ pottery of Malta is strongly individual, but none-the-less it shows more than a casual resemblance to contemporary Sicilian pottery. In that island the Stentinello impressed pottery was succeeded by wares decorated in the San Cono style, which seems to be basically a development of the Stentinello wares, though this explanation is not entirely satisfactory. The San Cono, like the Zebbuġ, style of decoration is based on narrow, but deeply cut bands,

63

the patterns being made up of from one to four of these lines running parallel and often bordered with dots. Wavy lines, and bands filled with dots also occur. A number of shapes are also common to the two, notably a small shouldered bowl with high strap-handle and a small ovoid jar. A fragment of a shallow bowl with a pedestal base from Malta is strikingly like one found at Predio Iozza in Sicily, and the Maltese strap-handles also have exact parallels in Sicily. On the other hand, human figures never appear on the Sicilian wares, and the whole effect is much poorer. The influences that produced the similarities may have come from the Maltese side, since the Maltese culture was developing vigorously at this time, whereas the aboriginal Neolithic culture of Sicily was in full decline owing to the appearance there at this time of new groups of immigrants from southern Italy and a little later from Greece and the Aegean with quite different cultural backgrounds.

As already hinted, however, the yellow-faced wares and those with painted decoration which are found in Malta at this time seem certainly to owe their inspiration to influence from abroad. People using painted pottery had early established themselves in south-east Italy, where their new wares gradually superseded the old impressed pottery, as they did also in the settlements in the Lipari islands on the north coast of Sicily. In late Stentinello times painted pottery gained a foothold in north-east and east Sicily, where it is found mixed in the same deposits with developed impressed pottery. The Sicilian painted pottery is pretty well identical with the south-east Italian variety, and it probably served as the model for the Maltese experiments with this technique of decoration—only to the extent of suggesting the use of paint, and the general colour scheme, however, since as we have seen the shape of the vases and the patterns used were purely Maltese.

The painted wares reached Sicily relatively late, and inspired the Maltese experiments even later, for they were already going or had already gone out of fashion in the other areas by this time. In southern Italy, the Lipari islands and Sicily they were succeeded by pottery covered with a mono-chrome red slip, which seems to have developed out of them by some change of fashion. This type of pottery has been christened 'Diana' ware by Dr Bernabò Brea, after a site in Lipari where he has found great quantities of it. It seems to take the place of the San Cono wares in the Mt Etna region of north-east Sicily, and fragments of the unmistakable trumpet-ended lugs which formed its normal handles have occasionally been found in Malta. There are less than a dozen in all—three or four from Mġarr, a couple from the Santa Verna temple in Gozo, and one from the Ġgantija temples in the same island, where it was found in the 1954 excavations in a mixed deposit of pottery of the third and fourth phases. The vases of which these handles formed a part must have been imported into Malta, as also was the small flake of the volcanic glass obsidian found with pottery of the third phase at Mġarr during the same 1954 excavations. The obsidian must have come from the Lipari islands, and it is quite likely that the Diana-type vases came from there too. Bernabò Brea has been able to work out a degeneration series of these Diana-type lugs in Lipari, and it is of interest to note that the Maltese examples would all come early in this series.

But connections with countries further afield than Sicily and the Lipari islands are suggested by some of the other relics of the third phase. For the inspiration which produced the monumental façade of the larger Mġarr temple, if it was really derived from abroad, we must look north and west to other regions in which megalithic architecture was being developed, such as France or Spain. The shell button with V-perforation *Fig. 8e* from Zebbuġ points in the same direction, since in all these areas this type of button was in vogue. Even more fascinating, though more puzzling, is the small statue-head from Zebbuġ. Plate 48

In a general way this recalls the carved stelae known as 'statue- menhirs' which are common in the earlier second millennium B.C. in some parts of southern France, as also in northern Italy (though some of the latter evidently date from much later, as probably do some recently discovered examples from Corsica). We find parallels for this remarkable object not only in the West, however; it has also some resemblance to the face carved on a stelae found by the American excavators some years ago in the first city of Troy, and in at least one detail—the repre- sentation of the mouth by a dot with a vertical line below it— it is comparable to pottery 'plank-idols' of the early Bronze Age from Cyprus. The exact significance, if any, of these far-flung resemblances provides a complex problem, to which we shall return in later chapters. For the moment it is enough that they exist.

It is still extremely difficult to give any dates in terms of years for the earlier phases which we can distinguish in terms of changing fashions in pottery and other materials of the develop- ing Maltese culture. The foreign connections give us a relative dating in terms of the culture-sequence in neighbouring lands, but the dating for these latter is often so controversial that this does not get us much nearer to a secure absolute date. It is therefore only possible to hazard a guess on one's own personal interpretation of the evidence. Mine would be that the third phase in Malta was reached at about the beginning of the second millenium B.C., when the culture had already been developing for some few hundred years in its island fastness. It is at about this time that rapid and important technological and economic developments began to take place in the cultures of Greece and the Aegean, that were to have far-reaching consequences in the West, including Malta. The rather tenuous connections with the Eastern Mediterranean which have been hinted at above might perhaps have something to do with the first intimations of the coming influence.

The fourth phase (D) which can be distinguished in the development of the Maltese temple-culture is in many ways the most crucial in its history. It is at this point that the prehistoric Maltese really begin unmistakably to surpass their neighbours in level of achievement. The ultimate causes of this phenomenon are obscure, as they generally are when such cultural efflorescences take place. There is a certain amount of evidence as to a few possible contributing factors, and this may be discussed and argued about, but it remains true that the cultural result is greater than the sum of these factors would have led us to expect.

After this, it may seem strange to say that the pottery style by which the phase was distinguished is in many ways the most insular, and shows the least sign of outside influence of them all. Yet this is the case. The majority of the shapes and the ware itself are fairly clearly descended from the pottery of the preceding phases. The decoration, though the applied technique is somewhat different, derives its general syntax fairly exactly and its patterns in a more general way from the repertoire of the preceding phases.

The new technique of pottery decoration consisted in scratching the outline of the patterns lightly on the surface of the vase after firing, instead of cutting deeply into it. Patterns made in this way appear to be less visible than those of the previous periods, but this is because the scratched lines were merely intended to hold in place blocks of red paste, which constituted the actual pattern visible to the eye on the finished vase. Often this colouring matter has been worn away, so that only the scratched pattern remains, but in some cases it has survived, in whole or in part, to warn us of what we must supply by imagination in the other cases. The red paste was applied in broad panels, as well as narrow lines; this is evident from examples on which it has survived, and from the fact that where the paste has disappeared, areas outlined by single lines

Plate 39
Fig. 10

are often completely filled up with a net of criss-cross lines whose purpose was to help the colouring matter to adhere to the highly polished surface.

This new decoration was probably intended as a substitute for the painted decoration which was attempted in the previous phase (perhaps not with entirely satisfactory results). At any rate the painted decoration goes out again entirely. On some fragments of light-faced ware from Kordin III, which may constitute early experiments with the new technique, the effect is almost identical with that of the old painted wares. The colouring of the pottery in this phase is, however, generally rather dark. Dark-grey and black is most common, though various shades of brown, especially a purplish- or reddish-brown are fairly frequent, and even orange and yellow occur. Many vases are mottled.

Fig. 10b, lower half of vase

For purposes of decoration, the field of the vase is generally divided into four panels, as before. These panels are filled with patterns, among which predominates the so-called 'comet' motif; this generally consists of two curved lines converging at one end. Round the point where they meet a small circle is often drawn. Sometimes the 'tail' of the comet consists of only one line, though two or more are customary. This pattern is foreshadowed by a similar one which occurs on some vases of phase B (see p. 50), and there are one or two instances of something like it in phase C too. The arrangement of this decoration is remarkably consistent. Generally a horizontal line runs round the vase just below the rim. Then come the panels with their interlocking comet patterns, filling most of the visible surface. Most of the vases of this phase again have rounded bases, with at most a little concave circular dimple (omphalos) at the centre to enable them to stand upright. The bases are also filled with comet patterns, often in a 'free-field' style. A certain number of vases found in 1955 in the already mentioned rock-tombs on Xemxija heights, however, have the main field of the vase filled with chequer-board patterns, in which the squares are alternately plain and cross-hatched (for the application of colouring matter). These vases can be safely assigned to this phase because, among other things, their rounded bases are covered with comet-patterns. About the significance of the chequer-board patterns we shall have more to say later.

Fig. 10a–c

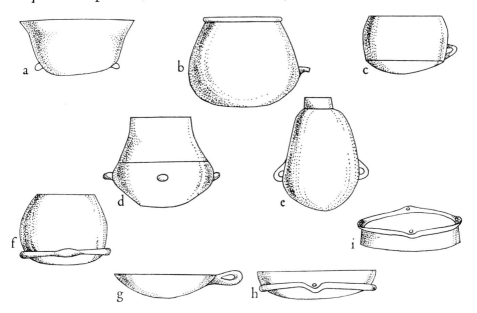

Fig. 9   Pottery shapes of phase ID. Not to scale

Among the shapes current in the vases of this phase are some new ones, though many are continued from the preceding phase. Large, bag-shaped bowls still continue to be made, with massive horizontal lug-handles set either on the rim or low on the body. A simple open bowl with everted rim and two elongated lugs set low on the body is common, as are squat jars with flattened ovoid bodies and conical necks. The

Fig. 9b

Fig. 9a

latter generally have four small knobs set on the shoulder, each surrounded by elaborate decoration. Other shapes include shallow dishes with a slightly convex base, around the top of which runs a beading pinched out at intervals and pierced with four string-holes at equal distances apart, shallow platters with a single oval handle on the rim, shouldered cups with a V-shaped handle (the ancestors, these, of a type of bowl that assumes great importance in the next and last phase), and ovoid, neckless jars with a heavily thickened rim (these last only known from fragments). As in the earlier phases, large storage jars are only known from small fragments, which makes it difficult to discover their shape. However, several sherds show the presence of a vase with a broad conical neck and a heavy lug-handle on its swelling—possibly the ancestor of the 'amphorae' which are well-known from reconstructed examples in the next phase. There is one reconstructed example of a jar

with a short conical neck and elongated ovoid body, having two stout lug-handles at its widest point. This, like the smaller pots, was finished by polishing and covered with scratched decoration of the usual type.

The Xemxija tombs have added several new shapes to the known repertoire of this phase. Most important are the vases with chequer-board decoration. These are all near-spherical in shape, with a thickened rim, and, about three-quarters of the

way down the body, a horizontal beading or cordon of clay pierced at the four quarters with vertical string-holes. This cordon divides the part decorated with chequer-board patterns from that which has comet-patterns. Next in importance are covers, of various sizes and types, but some at least clearly

descendants of the old cylindrical covers of phase two. The most common type resembles a shallow dish inverted. The old clumsy lugs have gone, to be replaced by the string-hole-pierced beading or cordon so favoured in this phase, and they are decorated with comet-patterns. A type of flat-based open bowl with two lugs set opposite each other on the rim recalls similar bowls current in the third phase, whilst another small flat-based bowl or cup anticipates a shape which was to become extremely common at the transition from phase D to phase E.

cp. Fig. 11a

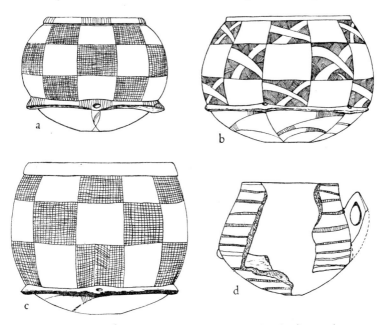

Fig. 10   Pottery of phase ID from the Xemxija tombs, a, b and c from tomb 3, d from tomb 5. Height of a 4 in., others to scale

As has been indicated, the string-hole lug in some form continues to be the most common type of handle on the pottery of this phase. Even the partly-pierced lug continues on some bag-shaped bowls. Some of them, however, take on more precise and less heavy and clumsy shapes than heretofore. Some of the tubular lug-handles show a curious feature, namely the pushing-in of the wall of the vase at the back of the lug, giving rise to a sort of semi-subcutaneous handle which is

71

Fig. 9c

further developed in the next stage (phase E). True handles in this phase are found only on the shouldered bowls, and even these seem to have been evolved from lugs rather than from the strap-handles of phase C. They are pointed, being of a more or less symmetrical V-shape, and in an adapted form they will become an elegant and common type in the next and last phase.

The pottery of this phase (D), which has such a local air about it, is found on many types of site, but is chiefly associated with temple buildings often of surprising size and elaborateness. Nothing short of a revolution comes about in the temple architecture during this time, and it is difficult to think of it as due merely to indigenous development. Some of the monuments that can be dated to this phase as a result of the excavations carried out in all the main temples in 1954, are still very much on the old style, both as to size, which is still moderate, and ground plan, though changes have occurred in the method of construction. Examples of this are the best preserved structure in
Figs. 13, 4, 3
the Kordin III complex and the small, badly preserved eastern building at Tarxien. In other cases, however, the buildings have become truly monumental in size, and their
Fig. 1 (11, 14)
Fig. 17 (1, 2)
Plate 13
ground plans have become more developed and complex. The best examples of this are the Ġgantija in Gozo and Ħaġar Qim, near Qrendi, in Malta. At both these sites all the buildings in the complex have been shown to belong to this phase, since fragments of its characteristic pottery were found in the lowest levels and in and under the foundations of walls at whatever points these were explored. Pottery of this phase has also been found in the Hypogeum, in rock-cut tombs and natural caves.

Though such large complexes of buildings survive from this phase there is unfortunately little in the way of portable material which we can associate with its pottery in any certain way. Some shell pendants, V-perforated buttons and miniature greenstone axes found in tomb 5 at Xemxija may equally well belong to the following phase, since pottery of both types abounded in this tomb. However, it may be presumed that a proportion of the implements of stone and bone, and the beads and amulets of stone, bone and shell found in the temples and rock tombs were made at this time. Whether any of the sculpture or the carvings found there go back as far as this is debatable. Nevertheless, there are one or two very primitive models of human heads having some features in common with types of figurine current in the Aegean which might date from this phase, though it cannot be proved at present.

The pattern of overseas connections which we can trace or infer from the material of phase D shows some significant changes from the earlier one. First of all, connections with Sicily, hitherto so important, cease, or at any rate cease to be reflected in the material though such raw materials as flint may still be imported. The reason for this is not far to seek. Sicily, formerly the home of a closely related culture, and the place whence the colonists had originally come to the Maltese islands, was now itself in the hands of new colonists with different cultural traditions; they had come from far away, from Greece and the Aegean, driven thence perhaps by the troubles and growing pains attending the birth of what was to grow into the Mycenean civilization. At any rate no connection can be traced between the Maltese pottery and the painted wares of the new inhabitants of Sicily, nor is there any trace there of monuments at all resembling the megalithic temples. The exuberant and somewhat bizarre patterns of the Maltese pottery of the fourth phase are in general highly individual, but the technique used has some significant parallels abroad, as have the chequer-board patterns on the vases from Xemxija. In France, Sardinia, northern and south-eastern Italy we find the technique of decorating pottery with scratched patterns over-laid with coloured paste in vogue, and in at least two of them, France and south-eastern Italy, the chequer-board pattern is used. In all these areas we may suspect that the technique owes its origin to an attempt to reproduce the effect of painted pottery, and may therefore have been developed independently in each. In south-eastern Italy, however, besides the technique itself and the chequer-board patterns, we can note also certain shapes closely resembling some of those used in Malta, most notably the conical-necked jars known in Italy as 'vasi a tocco' and nearly spherical vases like those with the chequer-board patterns in Malta. This may suggest at least some influence coming to Malta from Apulia, where the scratched wares co-existed with painted ones, though it must have been at best only a superficial one. The relative dating also presents problems, though recent work in south-eastern Italy suggests that both scratched and painted pottery may have survived there much longer than was once thought.

A sherd with a peculiar handle of a type known as 'nose-bridge' which was found at the Ġgantija may belong to a pot imported from the Lipari islands. It belongs to a type current in the culture that followed that of the red Diana ware there, which would fit well chronologically, though unfortunately its context in Malta is not absolutely certain. Apart from the rather dubious question of the idols and figurines, Aegean influence on Malta at some time during this period is mani-fested by a change of building technique that is extremely striking, but the discussion of this must be left until the detailed discussion of the architecture in the next chapter.

At the end of phase D the Aegean influences attribut-able to contacts with the explorers and traders of the Creto-Mycenean world, which have already shown themselves in the architecture, begin to permeate the whole of the Maltese culture and to leaven it in a most remarkable way. Among other things, its effect was to produce the pottery style by which the fifth phase (phase E) of the Maltese temple-culture can be defined. Once again there is a strong element of continuity to be seen, despite the new elements that appear. The ware, with a few exceptions, is technically similar to that of earlier phases, though even better fired and finished generally than in phase D, and some shapes can be traced through, though these are nearly always altered in the direction of greater precision of form and line. The technique of scratched decoration is developed and continued on a large proportion of the pottery.

At the same time, however, there is a far greater richness and diversity in the pottery of this phase than in that of any of the preceding ones. Many new types of vase appear, and a number of quite new decorative techniques come into use. The general effect produced by this pottery is remarkably sophisti‑ cated, and in this it is by no means an exception among the aspects of the culture of this phase which have survived. Besides the accomplished architecture of the temples belonging to this phase, and the inner halls of the Hypogeum, the many works of sculpture, relief‑carving and smaller amulets and trinkets that can be assigned to it make much the same impression. In stark contrast to this are certain other aspects such as, for example, the tool‑kit in use, which remains remark‑ ably backward and primitive. Antler picks and wedges and limestone mallets seem to have sufficed for stone‑cutting and excavating operations. Very few hard‑stone axes have been found, though axe‑amulets are common. Perhaps this was due   Plate 82 to the difficulty of obtaining suitable pieces of stone, which would have to be imported. Flint was imported and used to   *Fig. 12* make long, fine blades, and scrapers, as was obsidian; though   Plate 83 to judge from the finds, this latter material was not worked with any conspicuous success. Bone needles and borers are common, and a bone gouge was found in the Hypogeum, but this practically completes the exiguous catalogue of tool‑types. This poverty of equipment makes the successes of the Maltese civilization all the more remarkable.

To return for a while to the pottery, the most common type is a development of the scratched ware of phase D, but the

Plate 44 patterns are very different. The basic pattern which characterizes this phase is a kind of graceful volute enclosed in a semicircle. In a sense it could be claimed that this was evolved from the comet-patterns of the preceeding phase, since examples of patterns apparently intermediate between the two are known, but this would only be a half-truth. The occurrence of this type of volute pattern in other areas, and particularly very close parallels on some of the pottery from Crete, make it virtually certain that the 'evolution' here is only apparent, or at least that it took place under strong influence from abroad. There are elaborate variants of this basic motif, branched patterns that often become extremely complex and sometimes suggest stylized vegetable motives. Early in the phase a 'fringe' of short hair-like lines is often added to each line of the pattern. Later the background of the pattern is often covered with dots.

The range of other incised patterns represented on the pottery of the fifth phase is considerable. The true spiral, as opposed to the volute-pattern which has often been wrongly called spiral, is relatively rare, and when it does occur is usually provided with a dotted background. All the pots on which it is found seem to belong to a very advanced stage of the phase. Other patterns are bands of opposed semicircles, or ogival patterns, the space between them being filled up with cross- or vertical hatching, interlocked arcs of circles, arcs forming a kind of leaf-shaped motif, and branched patterns of all kinds based on the volute. Only one rectilinear pattern is at all common, a simple pattern of criss-cross lines forming lozenges. There is also a kind of stylized 'tree' or 'fern' pattern, whilst one sherd has a design which has been thought to represent ashlar masonry. A few pieces are decorated with designs representing animals, Plates 75, 74, 73 cattle, sheep or goats, snakes, birds, and in one instance what *Fig. 22* appears to be a rapid 'sketch from life' of a rather corpulent dancing girl in action! The latter was probably not part of the decoration of a whole pot, but was drawn on a sherd.

The scratched patterns are generally drawn with a firm hand, but sometimes so lightly as to be all but invisible without the incrustation of red ochre which they were intended to hold in place, as in the previous phase. In one case a pedestalled vase was thought to be undecorated until it was being drawn for the Survey, when, the light falling on it from a favourable angle, it was seen to be covered with an elaborate curvilinear design.

The appearance of a number of other decorative techniques in this phase comes as a distinct surprise. Like the painted decoration of phase C, they seem to have been mostly imitated from types in vogue in other areas. Two of the most common of these techniques, applied in many instances to vases of the finest type, are decoration by means of applied circular studs of clay (sometimes called 'hobnail' decoration), and 'jabbed' decoration, which consists of ovate marks made in the leather-hard clay of the pot by prizing it up with a spatula or flint blade. Half of the mark consists of the small pit made in the surface, the other half of the clay from it which is now raised above the general level of the surface. Both these techniques were intended to produce a similar effect, for in both cases the surface of the vase was covered with white paste so that only the raised patches, circular studs or lentoid spots of raised clay would be visible, on the same level as the surface of the paste. This paste has now for the most part worn away, and it can be seen that the surface of the vase, originally polished all over, like the scratched wares, was cut away and roughened over the whole area to be covered by the decoration, probably for the purpose of giving a better hold for the paste. A similar effect to that obtained by jabbing was sometimes produced by leaving small lentoid portions of the original surface at regular intervals. Jabbing was most commonly applied as an all-over decoration to small, flat-bottomed dishes, and occasionally to small biconical jars or parts of biconical bowls. Studs, on the other

Plates 41, 42

Fig. 11e, b

77

hand, were employed primarily on carinated bowls, sometimes as an all-over decoration, but sometimes as a filling for curvilinear patterns of the type usual on the scratched wares, which are then outlined by deep incisions.

Somewhat akin to the two types of decoration just described is the technique, generally applied only to a type of reddish-coloured carinated bowl, of covering the surface with a series of broad grooves before the pot is fired. These grooves were most commonly arranged vertically, though more rarely a kind
Fig. 28
of hurdle-pattern is formed by alternating panels of vertical and horizontal grooves. This decoration, like that of the jabbed and studded types, was generally, if not always, completed by the application of white paste.

All the types of decoration so far discussed were applied to vases from the common range of shapes to which scratched decoration was also proper. There are, however, several types of decoration making their first appearance in this phase, which are applied only to a series of large and small storage jars,
whose shapes do not occur in the normal range. The ware itself and its finish are also new in Malta. It is coarser than the traditional type of ware in use there, and is fired to a reddish or purplish colour. The surface is smoothed, but neither slipped nor polished. Often the vases made of this ware seem to have been built up of rings or spirals of clay. The largest of the storage
Plate 45
jars have an all-over rusticated decoration which resembles overlapping scales. These seem sometimes to have been pinched out of the wet clay with the finger-tips, sometimes to have been applied separately as small pieces of clay and moulded to shape. The smaller jars usually have four long spines of clay applied
Plate 47
vertically on the shoulder, the spaces between being filled by shell-like patterns made by smearing the wet clay with the finger-tip. The lower part of the body of the vase is filled with vertical fluting made by the same method. There may also be a few minor applied knobs of clay just below the rim.

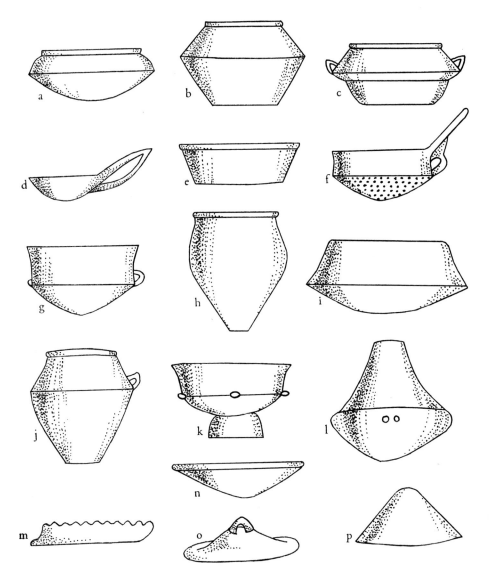

Fig 11   Pottery shapes of phase IE. Not to scale

Plate 73

Applied decoration was sometimes, like scratched decoration, used to make (generally rather crude) plastic representations of animals. Among these are bulls' heads, sows (twice), birds (once between a pair of horns, probably a symbolic device), and even crude human faces. Generally these are on coarse vases, though one representation of three human heads occurs on a fragment of a fine slip-ware bowl, while in one other case an applied spine on an unusually fine slip-ware jar was converted into a face by the addition of two almond-shaped eyes scratched on either side of it. Another interesting feature of this sherd is that it has shell patterns like those described above, but executed in scratched technique. Its shape, however, appears to be that of a coarse-ware jar. It may be added here that occasionally the plastic scale-patterns are applied to fine-ware bowls. It is impossible to draw an absolutely hard and fast line between the types.

Finally, there is an unusual technique, which is used rarely to obtain an effect similar to that of the red-encrusted scratched patterns, but probably a good deal more permanent. This is the method of clay inlay, and it was used on carinated and biconical bowls to produce volute-patterns and even true spirals. The pattern was first marked out, and then the surface of the vase was cut away over the area occupied by it, and the material thus removed was replaced by clay to which had been added an admixture of some red colouring matter. The pot was then burnished and fired, after which the outline of the pattern, which sometimes tended to get a little blurred, was emphasized by deep incisions, and these were in turn filled with white paste. Great care seems to have been lavished on these magnificent vases, but unfortunately no complete example of them has survived. The highly polished slip is always of a beautiful honey-brown colour, and the final effect must have been very striking.

It has been said that the range of shapes in this phase is

very large. There is one shape, however, which is more common than all the others put together, and provides a kind of keynote. This is the carinated bowl, generally having a single triangular handle which stands on the carination, and is balanced on the other side of the vase by a little semicircular button. These bowls are clearly derived from the shouldered bowls of the previous phase. The handle has become asymmetrical, and the shape is more precise, but otherwise there is little change. Fragments of these bowls are found in such numbers on the temple-sites as to suggest that they were used to bring food offerings and then ritually broken to prevent their being desecrated by further use. Also indigenous are such shapes as that of the large 'amphorae' with twin tunnel-handles, shallow bowls, flat-bottomed dishes, small ovoid pots, and even the curious 'Saflieni bowls', which are quite probably remote descendants of the bell-necked jar of phase C. Some of them have metope or chequer-board designs, and seem likely to date from the very beginning of phase E or the end of phase D. Quite new, however, are biconical bowls, footed bowls, high-handled ladles and strainer-bowls with handles attached to a tall triangular plaque which rises from the rim (these handles are strikingly paralleled on small cups of the San Ippolito culture of Sicily). New too is the shape of a great biconical jar, about 3 ft high, perhaps the finest complete example of the ancient Maltese potter's art, with its fine incised and encrusted decoration, enormous triangular handle and four small tunnel-handles (probably for securing a cover).

Handles in this phase are very stereotyped and belong mostly to a few well-defined classes. Apart from the curious handles on the strainer-bowls there are three main types: first, the triangular handles, common on the carinated bowls, and other vases; then, the tunnel-handles, now fully developed from the semi-subcutaneous lugs of phase four, and used chiefly on 'amphorae' but also on the great jar just mentioned; and finally, much

Fig. 11g

Fig. 9c

Fig 11l; Plate 46
Fig. 11e

Fig. 11i; Plate 40

Plate 39; *Fig. 11a*
Fig. 11b, d, f

Fig. 11j
Plate 43

rarer, triangular strap-handles, which form an element in the strainer-bowl handles, but which are sometimes used alone. More than one of these handle-types may occur on a single pot. 'Saflieni bowls' are exceptional in this phase in having lugs, sometimes taking the form of small pierced knobs, but at others formed into beautifully finished trumpet lugs. Covers like shallow dishes turned upside down, which are a special feature of this phase, have sometimes a peculiar type of wishbone handle.

Fig. 11 o, p

Pottery of phase E is known from a very large number of sites and was found in such great quantities in the Hypogeum and most of the main temple-sites that for a long time it prevented that of any of the earlier phases from being recognized. The two complexes whose surviving buildings belong mainly to this phase are Tarxien and Mnajdra, which lies on the coast very near Ħaġar Qim; but there are a few minor monuments dating solely or mainly from this phase, notably Buġibba, well-known for its carvings, on the east side of St Paul's Bay. The inner halls of the Hypogeum, with their paintings and elaborate carving, also seem to date from it. At Tarxien about ninety-seven per cent of the material found in the older excavations dated from this phase.

Fig. 1 (10)

Fig. 1 (12, 13)

The external relations of the Maltese culture during this phase of its cultural apogee have been hinted at once or twice above, and they will be fully dealt with in later chapters. Suffice it here to say that the pottery shows clearly in the patterns of its decoration that the culture was in some sort of contact with the Aegean civilizations, with Crete at the end of the Middle Minoan and beginning of the Late Minoan periods, and with the early phase of the Mycenean culture of the mainland. Perhaps the somewhat 'metallic' shapes of many of the types in this phase are a further reflection of contact with the Aegean and knowledge of metal vases. Nevertheless, the Maltese pottery, despite the remarkable precision of its shapes, continues to be hand-made, and there is no indication that metal was used.

The appearance of the studded and plastic types of decoration in this phase hint at connections with the lands of the Western Mediterranean. Decoration of this type is known in south-eastern and eastern Italy, where, however, it is difficult to say exactly when it began. They are also known in southern France and parts of Spain and Portugal, as also is the grooved decoration of 'channelled' technique. The latter is particularly well-known in southern France, where it belongs to the advanced 'Chal-colithic' period, and is known as the Fontbouïsse style. Tunnel-handles seem to have been developed in Malta, but are also found in Sardinia and south-western France, where they occur on pots decorated with channelled lines like those of the Fontbouïsse style, but making different patterns. They are probably contemporary with them. The connections in the Western Mediterranean indicated by the pottery are therefore with the same areas as in the fourth phase.

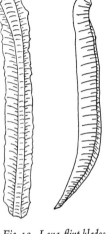

Fig. 12 Long flint blades from the Tarxien temples. Length of curved blade 4 in., other to scale

It is still difficult to give exact dates for this phase, but it seems likely from various indications that it covered the middle of the second millennium B.C. The Myceneans had established their base in the Lipari islands by the middle of the 16th century B.C., and the Cretan connections of the Maltese culture would seem to date from slightly earlier than this. Thus it seems likely that the fifth phase was in progress before 1600 B.C., while from various other considerations it seems unlikely to have ended before 1500 B.C. This would agree well enough with the relatively vague ideas we have of the dating of the Fontbouïsse phase in France.

At the end of phase E the culture of the temple-builders mysteriously disappears from Malta. We have now traced its complete history as reflected in the stages distinguishable in the pottery, and may go on to consider some of the more striking and interesting aspects of this strange culture.

83

CHAPTER III

Temples and Tombs

THE MOST INTRIGUING and impressive remains left by the earliest Maltese are undoubtedly the great megalithic temples which still rear their gnarled and weather-worn fronts at a number of points on the islands. To these we must add the great catacomb or Hypogeum of Hal Saflieni, discovered in 1901; in some respects it is even more impressive than the finest of the temples. As a result of the recent Survey it is now at last possible to give a connected account of these monuments, showing their gradual development, their interrelations and their place in the life of the ancient Maltese. That this is so is to a large extent because of the establishment of the five phases of ceramic development outlined in the previous chapter, since it is these that have made it possible to give a relative dating in terms of the sequence to the various buildings and portions of buildings in each complex, and so to work out a scheme of architectural development based on something more secure than the mere typology of ground-plans. The architectural sequence thus arrived at shows a develop- ment from the small and simple to the large and complex such as might have been expected and as might have been deduced from the building remains themselves (though in fact the very opposite conclusion was arrived at by Zammit and the Italian, Ugolini). The point is, that such a typological sequence could work equally well starting from either end, and it is only the pottery-sequence proved by stratigraphy and checked at various points by connections with foreign sequences that enables us to be certain as to which end is the right one to start from.

About thirty sites of buildings of this type are known, though less than a dozen are represented by substantial remains at the present day. They vary tremendously in size and com/ plexity, from sites covering only a few square yards to such ones as Tarxien, whose main group of buildings covers an area of some 6,500 sq. yards. The stones of which they are constructed show an equal range of variation from rubble and small boulders to huge slabs like one incorporated in the outer wall of Ḥaġar Qim which is 22 ft long and weighs many tons. The latter is the largest used in any of the temples, though some others are not so very much inferior.

Fig. 18

Plate 13 (extreme left)

I have been referring to these buildings as temples, and so they are, but there has not always been general agreement on this point, for they are temples of a very peculiar kind. Many of the features of their construction—the monumental façade, the rooms arranged on either side of a backbone of courts and corridors, the occurence of small rooms and niches which some/ times have to be entered by means of a window/like opening or 'porthole' cut in a large slab, the very use of megalithic slabs itself—have suggested to many students that they were in some way connected with the collective tombs, often also megalithic in construction, which occur in many areas of the Western Mediterranean and Western Europe generally. Nevertheless, they are not tombs, for no burials have ever been found in them (except at Tarxien, where they occur as the result of a re/use of the building by later people). Burials belonging to the first Maltese culture have so far been found only in natural caves, rock/cut tombs, and the great catacomb of Hal Saflieni. In the following account of the development of the megalithic and rock/cut monuments, it will become clear that it is possible to reconcile these apparently conflicting facts, and, while showing that the former really are temples, to explain satisfactorily why they have many features apparently more proper to tombs.

Figs. 13, 17

Plates 14, 19

The earliest of the surviving megalithic monuments is the one at Mġarr, which, as was mentioned in the previous chapter, consists of two parts, dating from the second and third phases

Fig. 1 (2)

Plate 2

Fig. 1 (4, 3)

Fig. 13 (1)

(B and C) respectively. No monument exists which can be assigned to the first phase, though the fact that a few sherds of impressed ware of phase A have turned up on the site of the Mġarr temples in Malta, and those of Xewkija and Santa Verna in Gozo, may indicate that some sort of building was in existence on those sites even as early as that. At Mġarr, the smaller of the two buildings, though it appears to be simply an annexe to the larger, is in fact the older. It was built of quite small stones, which could easily be robbed; hence little survived at the time of excavation except the ground plan. The walls have now been built up with rubble to a height of two or three feet, but the appearance of the monument is very unimpressive. Nevertheless, this extremely tatty little structure is of the greatest importance for the elucidation of the origin and meaning of the Maltese temples.

It is more or less oval in shape, with an entrance in one of the long sides in the form of a short corridor flanked by the remains of six upright slabs, three on each side. The interior is divided up in a curious way into several recesses or chambers arranged around a central area. The two largest of these lie to right and left after one has passed through the entrance, and are roughly horseshoe shaped. A third similar, but rather smaller, recess lies opposite the entrance, and off this opens on the right a still smaller semicircular chamber, once entered through a small trilithon doorway, which survived when the building was excavated in the mid-1920's but has since been destroyed. This building, measuring about 35 ft by 25 ft over-all, contains in embryo most of the main features of what was to become the architectural unit from which the Maltese temple-complexes were built up, the group of chambers centring about a central spine composed of courts and corridors. There is no trace of a façade, though we cannot be sure that one never existed, since it would in any case have had to be removed when the larger monument was built on in phase three. Some support, however,

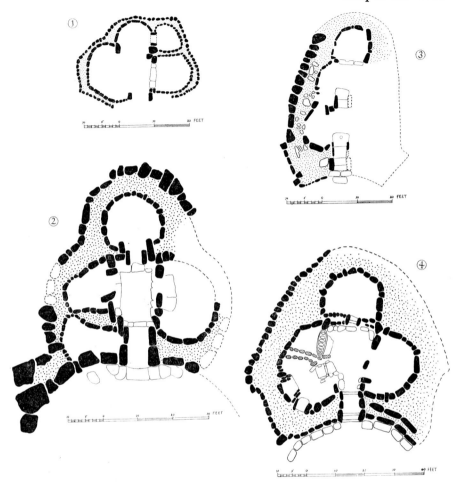

Fig. 13 Plans of the earlier types of temple-units. 1, 2 Ta Ḥaġrat, Mġarr, 3 Tarxien, 4 Kordin III. Various scales

is given to the idea that no façade ever existed by one of the finds made during the original excavations. This is a small piece of globigerina limestone carved to represent a building

87

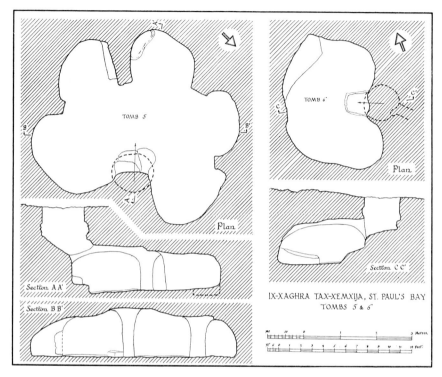

Fig. 14   Plans of tombs 5 and 6 at Xemxija

with a plan very like the one we are considering; here it is clear
that there was no façade.

Such are the remains of the earliest and most primitive built
monument in Malta, and very puzzling they are. The plan, for
instance, seems so odd and arbitrary, yet is obviously deliberately
chosen and followed. Much simpler shapes could surely have
been hit upon for a building in stone. One gets the irresistible
impression that an attempt is being made to reproduce something from another medium, so clumsy and all-adapted does
it seem. And this in fact may well be the case. Some recent
discoveries strongly suggest that it is, incidentally providing a

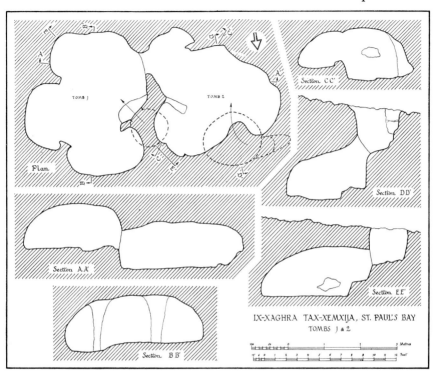

Fig. 15   Plans of tombs 1 and 2 at Xemxija

fairly satisfying explanation of the possible origin of the Maltese temples.

Mention has already been made of the five rock-cut tombs on the Xemxija Heights, excavated in 1955. This was the first well-preserved group of rock tombs dating from the temple-period to be recognized in Malta, and they have proved to be the key to the whole development of both the rock-cut and the built monuments of the Maltese islands. The basic form of these tombs, well illustrated by Numbers 3, 4 and 6, is a more or less kidney-shaped chamber, entered through a small circular 'porthole' at the bottom of a cylindrical pit. Variations

Fig. 1 (27)

Fig. 14, tomb 6

89

Fig. 15; Plate 32

Fig. 14, tomb 5

Fig. 13 (1)

Plate 33
Fig. 14, tomb 5

and elaborations of this plan are presented by Numbers 1, 2 and 5. The first two are joined together by a short corridor, though they have their own separate entrances of the usual form as well. Number 5 is larger than any of the others, being about 20 ft by 18 ft at its widest points, and part of the interior is divided into separate recesses by partitions formed by leaving portions of the rock standing out from the back wall of the chamber. Similar partitions are also a feature of tomb 1. A comparision of the plans of tomb 5 with that of the small building at Mġarr which has just been described shows a remarkable degree of resemblance between the two. If the Mġarr building represented an attempt to reproduce the shape of a rock-cut tomb like Xemxija 5 above ground, it would make sense. The basic kidney-shaped plan of the Xemxija tombs is natural enough for a chamber hollowed out of the rock, and if this be enlarged to cover more than a quite small area, screens or partitions of rock would have to be left, or others introduced, to support the roof. Thus the partitions between the recesses in tomb 5 were a structural necessity, reproduced arbitrarily in the Mġarr monument.

What prompted the early Maltese to begin reproducing their rock-cut monuments above ground we can only guess. The Xemxija chambers are collective tombs, in which the bones of a large number of individuals have been found in disorder, mixed with the bones of animals probably included as food offerings and the remains of pottery and other grave goods. No trace was found of human remains in the Mġarr monument, however, any more than in any of the other built monuments in the Maltese islands. If it was ever used as a tomb, it was certainly thoroughly cleared at an early date and converted to other uses. These, one can hardly doubt, were the same as those for which the later and more elaborate temples were constructed, namely the celebration of religious rites. But why should a building designed to be a shrine or temple imitate the form of a tomb? The answer is clear—only if the rites to be celebrated there have to do with the dead. That this was the case is confirmed by everything that we can learn about the religion of the ancient Maltese, and it can be further supported by calling in evidence from abroad. The collective rock-cut and megalithic tombs of Western Europe, whose close analogies with the Maltese monuments have already been referred to, are all in some degree shrines where rites for the propitiation of the ancestor-spirits were carried out, often in the area enclosed by a monumental concave façade, like those of the Maltese temples. In these collective tombs we frequently meet with representations of a female figure, a sort of personification of fertility (often thought of in primitive religion as being under the control of ancestor-spirits), comparable to the obese deity who plays such a large part in the later development of the Maltese cult.

We are thus provided with a credible explanation of the origin of temple-building, and of the tomb-like features of the temples. It is possible that the first Mġarr monument, or other similar monuments which have now disappeared, were themselves used as tombs at first, but they soon ceased to be so, and became entirely appropriated to the purposes of the religion which grew up out of the cult of the dead. The dead continued to be buried in natural or artificial caves, the latter sometimes, as in the case of the Hypogeum, of a very elaborate kind, and this custom was continued unchanged to the final disappearance of the temple-culture. Specialization of the kind developed in the Maltese monuments is not found in any other community of collective tomb-builders in Western Europe, though instances have been found, in Orkney and (probably) in western France, of a special variant of the normal monument being built for purely ritual purposes. A few fragments of pottery of types proper to phase B found in the Xemxija tombs show that some at any rate of these are as old as the Mġarr building though they continued in use until much later.

Although we cannot at present prove that rock-cut tombs are older than megalithic monuments in Malta, this is a fair presumption, since otherwise we should have to derive them from the built monuments, which would make no sense at all. We may still hope to find earlier ones some day, though this is not very likely, since rock-tombs were used and re-used in Malta for thousands of years, and most of the early ones have probably suffered this fate. The origin of the rock-cut tomb in the earliest Maltese culture is easy to guess, since collective burial in natural caves, such as may have taken place in the earliest times at Għar Dalam, and which is known also in later phases, would naturally give rise in time to the idea of making artificial caves, better adapted to requirements, by scooping out chambers in the soft rock of the islands. Thus the whole great process that ends with the Hypogeum and the great temple-complexes probably started in the dusky recesses of the Għar Dalam, a place already more than half filled with the remains of the extinct animals which once roamed there.

Once under way, the development of the temples and their differentiation from the tombs in form made rapid strides. The second monument at Mġarr is already very much more developed than the first, though it belongs only to the next phase. It is a good deal larger, the over-all dimensions being about 60 ft by 50 ft, and the parts are much more clearly articulated. The plan is that of three rooms grouped about a central rectangular court, forming a trefoil pattern, something like the shape of a clover-leaf. The front of the building is formed by a massive hollow façade of huge megalithic slabs, which encloses a semicircular area in front of the monument. This façade is fairly well preserved on the left-hand side, but the right-hand portion has suffered severely and only a part of it can now be seen. The entrance is in the middle of the façade. A flight of four steps leads into a short corridor formed by megalithic slabs. This, in turn, leads into the central court, an

Plate 1

Fig. 13 (2)

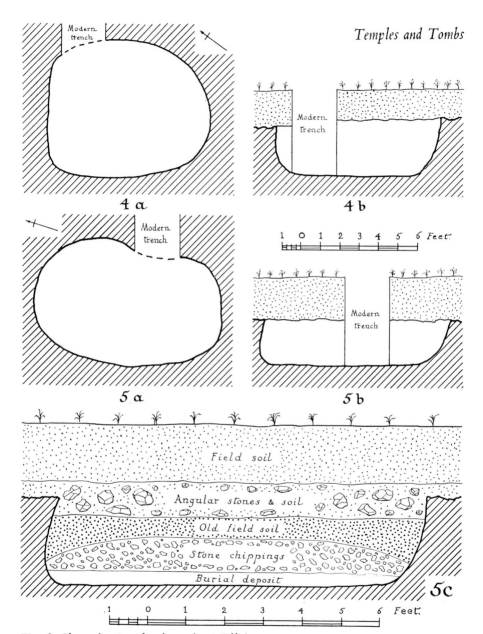

4 a

4 b

Modern trench

Modern trench

5 a

5 b

1 O 1 2 3 4 5 6 Feet

Modern trench

Modern trench

Field soil

Angular stones & soil

Old field soil

Stone chippings

Burial deposit

5c

1 O 1 2 3 4 5 6 Feet

Fig. 16   Plans and sections of tombs 4 and 5 at Zebbuġ

area surrounded by a low stone kerb, and off which open the various rooms. Those to right and left are more or less semi-circular, and are separated from the court by screens made of upright slabs, except where a gap is left to give entrance. In the case of the left-hand room, this gap is flanked by two Plate 4 massive portal stones. The rear room, which is almost circular, has a more complicated entrance, with two overlapping sets of portal stones forming a short corridor that widens towards the interior. The whole building is surrounded by a solid outer wall, the space between this and the walls of the rooms being filled up (as was the normal practice in all the Maltese mega-lithic buildings) with earth and rubble. At one point in the outer wall, just behind the rear room, is a doorway, flanked by two upright slabs, between which is a horizontal one serving as a threshold. This must have led into some kind of passage between the walls, no trace of which remains. The entrance to the smaller temple opens off the right-hand room, which in consequence is somewhat deformed.

Apart from the stones used for the façade and the corridors and portals, large megalithic slabs are not used in the con-struction of this monument. Both the inner and outer walls Plates 2, 4 were made by piling up rough slabs and boulders with no attempt at coursing. The material used throughout is the hard coralline limestone, which is relatively difficult to shape, and none of the stones show any signs of having been dressed. Despite the roughness of its construction, and despite much recent destruction, this building is still quite impressive, especially the monumental façade, the largest slab of which still stands nearly 12 ft high.

The two monuments just described are the only structures that can be assigned to the second and third phases, though a mound at Li Skorba, close by, from which megalithic blocks protrude, may cover ruins of similar age. When we come to the fourth phase, D, however, the case is altered, for we have a mass of very varied material which can be assigned to it. The most important structural advances in the history of the Maltese temple architecture fall within this phase and some of the most magnificent and imposing examples were built during it. Beginning with structures little more advanced than the Mġarr monument we have just discussed, it ends with monuments of great size and magnificence, and which in all essential respects have already reached the limit of their development.

An example of the first type can be found in the best preserved structure at the Kordin III site. It is a moderatesized monument, having a trefoil or cloverleaf plan like that of the larger Mġarr monument, though its dimensions are somewhat larger, its overall length being about 60 ft. The chambers are all horseshoeshaped in this monument, being separated from the paved central court, which is somewhat irregular in shape, by stone screens. The lefthand room, which is the biggest, was divided into two by a wall built subsequently to the original construction, in the larger of which, lying nearer the façade, a number of niches were also constructed at this time. The smaller compartment was separated from the central area by a long stone slab laid horizontally, in the top of which seven oval compartments have been hollowed out to a considerable depth. Whilst it is possible that these may have been made in ancient times for ritual purposes, it seems equally possible that they may have been made quite recently by Maltese peasants utilizing the slab as a surface on which to grind up the sherds of ancient pottery to be found on the site; this forms a muchprized ingredient of a cement called 'deffun' widely used for the roofing of houses. A large hollow has been worn in the huge threshold stone of the Ġgantija south building by the same agency.

The building just described is firmly dated to phase D, pottery of this phase being the latest found beneath the paving of the

Fig. 1 (5)
Fig. 13 (4)

central court and around the foundations of walls in excavations made here in 1954. As in the case of the Mġarr monument, walls are constructed chiefly of rough blocks and boulders though large slabs are used for corridors and portals. It is provided with a curved façade of large slabs and an outer wall, both of which it shares with a rather smaller and much destroyed building adjoining it on the right. The latter has a very primitive plan, more like that of the earlier Mġarr building but it is nevertheless dated to phase D by the pottery found therein. The Kordin trefoil represents some advance over the phase C monument at Mġarr in one notable respect: the large slabs of the façade, corridors, etc. show some signs of having been dressed. The area enclosed by the curved façade that fronted the two buildings just described was floored with cobbles. Another small trefoil building of this phase has been recognized and restored in the Mnajdra complex, though it had been almost destroyed. A small and much damaged building to the east of the main block at Tarxien also belongs to phase D though in plan it probably was closer to the huge monuments about to be described than to the small trefoils.

Fig. 13 (3)

Fig. 18

The next structure which it is of importance for us to consider in tracing the development of the Maltese temples is the complex known as the Ġgantija, in Gozo, which is in some ways the most impressive of the surviving monuments in the Maltese islands. It consists of two separate temples set side by side and joined together by a common outer wall. The south building, besides being much the larger, is almost certainly also the earlier of the two. Its walls survive in parts to a height of about 17 ft, and its outer wall is made of huge slabs, which include some of the largest ever used in the Maltese islands. In this building we meet once more (for the last time) the trefoil plan, reproduced on a much enlarged scale, but this time with a new innovation in the shape of a second and somewhat smaller pair of lateral chambers set in front of the first pair and

Fig. 1 (11)

Fig. 17 (1, 2)

Fig. 17 (1)

Plate 11

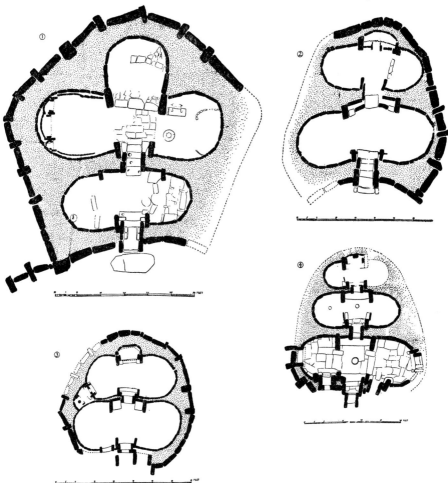

Fig. 17 Plans of the later types of temple-units. 1, 2 Ġgantija, 3 Mnajdra, north temple, 4 Tarxien, middle temple. Approx. over-all lengths (passage axis): (1) 110 ft, (2) 90 ft, (3) 70 ft, (4) 80 ft

communicating with it by means of a short passage. These two front rooms somehow have the air of being supplementary to the enormous trefoil which forms the core of the building; so that, whilst it was unfortunately not possible to prove this when

97

excavations were made here in 1954, it is tempting to believe that this outer portion, built on a lesser scale, was subsequently added for the purpose of adapting the original building to the requirements of an ever more complex ritual. This plan with two sets of lateral chambers is found in all later temples in Malta, but in all cases, including the north building at Ġgantija itself, the front pair of chambers is larger than the rear one. The only exception to this is found in Ġgantija South, which emphasizes the probability that here we have to do with an afterthought. This south building measures something like 100 ft in length by nearly as much again in breadth. The largest of the chambers is just under 30 ft across and nearly 35 ft long. Even the daring Maltese builders hesitated to attempt anything bigger than the two rear chambers of this edifice!

Fig. 17 (2)

The adjoining north building is smaller and less massively constructed, having an over-all length and breadth of only about 75 ft, although in plan, as already hinted, it shows a distinct advance. The individual chambers are more or less semicircular, as is usual in the later temples (Caruana rather clumsily coined the word 'hemicycles' to describe them!). The two front chambers of the south building have a similar plan and form a sharp contrast to the three distinctly horseshoe-shaped ones behind. In the north building the front chambers are appreciably larger than the rear ones, and it is also striking that here, as in almost all of the later temples, the rear chamber, which reached such gigantic proportions in the south building, has been reduced to a shallow recess in the rear wall of the building.

Plate 10

Certain ritual installations which are characteristic of the later Maltese temples make their first appearance at the Ġgantija. For instance, a pair of large 'altars', each consisting of a horizontal slab laid in a recess formed by upright slabs, are set one on each side of the entrance to the passage leading from the outer to the

inner chambers. These altars are found not only in the north
building, where they could be contemporary with the construction, but also in the front chambers of the south building,
where they are almost certainly a later addition, since one of
them is carved with a spiral pattern which must belong to
phase E.

The remaining installations are chiefly niches or tabernacles
formed of slabs, which are common in all the later temples. The
remains of one of these was found in the recess at the back of the
north building, and it was possible to show that it was not
part of the original construction, but was added at some later
date. In 1954 the packing of earth and stones which had been
put behind the niche at the time of its construction to fill the
space between the back of it and the wall of the temple was
investigated. It yielded a number of pieces of pottery of types
proper to phase E, whereas no pottery later than phase D was
found below the floors of the temple when trenches were cut
through them to bedrock.

Similar arrangements of niches or tabernacles, and other
installations were found in the south building, especially in the
right-hand chamber of the first pair (where they included a
'baetyl' shaped rather like a high-explosive shell) and in both
chambers of the back pair. They were also evidently added,
like the altars, subsequently to the original construction of the
edifice, probably during phase E, though this could not be
checked. These elaborate fittings have been very badly damaged
and in some cases their traces almost obliterated due to the fact
that the buildings were left open and unenclosed for just over a
century after the original excavations, until the land on which
they stand was acquired by the Government for the Museum
Department in 1933. A comparison of the interior as it stands
at the present day, with a painting of it by Brocktorff in 1827,
three years after the excavations, clearly shows the frightful
extent of this damage.

Plates 7, 8

Plate 10

Plates 7, 8

Plate 11

The outer wall that surrounds these two large buildings is constructed in a novel way not found at Mġarr. Instead of being composed of irregular boulders piled pell-mell on top of each other, the lower part comprises a series of huge slabs set on end. Generally, slabs set broadside-on alternate with pillar-like slabs set with their narrow sides outwards, though there are portions of the wall where pillar-slabs are not used. This technique becomes a regular feature of the outer walls of the later temples, since it obviously had a strengthening effect on the structure. Above the slabs the wall was continued by means of long blocks of stone laid in horizontal courses which incline gradually inwards. As many as three or four courses of these blocks survive at some points. The façade of the buildings is constructed in a similar fashion by piling blocks in courses above the uprights. At one point in the façade of the south building no less than five courses survive. The method of construction used for the inside walls, however, is still the old one, rough blocks of stone piled on top of each other. There is a noticeable tendency, however, to have a bottom course composed of larger blocks than are used for the upper parts. All the walls that are preserved to any height have a perceptible overhang, and this is particularly evident in the case of the rear chamber of the south building, where they are preserved to

Plate 9, on right

the greatest height. The significance of this evidence for the question of roofing will be considered later.

Plate 7

Slabs are employed in the interior only for corridors and the stones which partially divide the lateral chambers from the central space. It is interesting to notice that these slabs are often of globigerina limestone, and are dressed to an exact shape and sometimes ornamented with a decoration of holes drilled in rows all over the surface. The slabs used for the external walls, on the other hand, are rough and undressed, being of hard coralline limestone. Here we see the beginning of the deliberate use of the different types of limestone for different constructional purposes, which was to be a marked feature of the later architecture.

The two temples known as the Ġgantija stand on a hillside, facing down the slope. In front of them, however, stretches a more or less circular level platform about 100 ft in diameter. This is artificial, being built up of great boulders piled on top of one another, and kept from rolling down the hill by a massive megalithic retaining wall, parts of which are now covered by modern walling. This platform was examined in 1954, and was found to be an addition made in phase E. Beneath the boulders was a deposit of black earth 3 ft thick; the small area of this that was examined produced an enormous quantity of phase E pottery, and similar sherds were also found among the stones of the platform.

Fig. 28
Plate 74

Apart from the Ġgantija, one other great temple-complex was found to date in its entirety from the fourth phase. This is the one known as Ħaġar Qim, situated on the top of a rise near the village of Qrendi, whence it commands a fine view over the south coast of Malta and the sea beyond, in the midst of which the tiny island of Filfla forms a point of interest. Though one of the largest and most imposing of the megalithic monuments the Ħaġar Qim group has little more to tell us about the formal evolution of the Maltese temple. The main building is a con-fused mass of chambers and courts resulting from much desultory alteration and rebuilding of the original monument. It is difficult even now to say which, if any, of the surviving parts may belong to this original building, or what it may have been like. Even the evidence of pottery fails us here. Excavations were made in all parts of the complex in 1954, but beyond establishing that the whole process of building was completed within the limits of phase D they yielded little. Nevertheless, the Ħaġar Qim buildings, apart from their intrinsic interest, display a number of technical novelties in construction which makes it necessary to insert a brief description of them here.

Fig. 1 (14)

Plate 13

Besides the main group of structures, there are two minor buildings and traces of a third at Haġar Qim, but these need not concern us. The main block, seen from above, presents a curiously lopsided appearance, caused by its irregular growth on the south-west side. To what may originally have been a relatively normal building with two sets of chambers a fan-shaped arrangement consisting of four chambers of different shapes and sizes has been added. In the process the rear left-hand chamber of the regular building has been demolished and transformed into a broad passage leading from one part of the building to the other. We cannot be absolutely certain that this was the order of construction, but there is some evidence to support it, and it seems on general grounds most likely. At best, however, it is only a very over-simplified version of a complex process whose details it is impossible to recover. The regular portion of the building is entered from the south-east through a short passage set in the middle of a curved façade of the usual type. The first two chambers are unusual in being completely cut off from the central court by screens of slabs set on edge, and access can only be gained through window-like openings cut in two of these. The buildings also differ from the normal plan in that the place of the back recess is taken by a further short corridor leading out into the open area behind the building.

The rear recess which is missing here is supplied in the first of the built-on rooms; this lies beyond the left-hand chamber of the first pair, and faces in the opposite direction to the building just described. It has the air of having originally been built as a regular pair of chambers of the usual type, of which the right-hand one was subsequently destroyed, but the 1954 excavations here show that this is probably deceptive, and that it was built originally as it now stands, and is later than the building to the north-east. To the north-west of this chamber lie two more oval rooms, which may be entered either from the interior, or by separate entrances through the outer wall. Beyond the second of these rooms to the north lies a further enclosure, consisting this time of the usual two semicircular chambers on either side of a central space. The entrance to this area was from the north side, and a further passage on the south side, which perhaps once led into a further pair of chambers, is now blocked by the wall of the room beyond. Between the right-hand chamber of the last-mentioned pair and the destroyed left-hand rear chamber of the regular building is a curious area containing two small rooms filled with ritual installations of the niche-and-pillar type. This area was excavated in 1909 by Zammit, and the description of the pottery found leaves no doubt that they were constructed, or at least arranged, in phase E. They are the only pieces of construction in the building that can be dated as late as this phase.

This puzzling building, with its clear evidence of changes of plan, and its frequent reconstructions, all apparently carried out within a single chronological phase, is probably the most irregular in plan of all the major monuments. At the same time, although it is such a jumble, it is nonetheless one of the most striking pieces of architecture left by the ancient Maltese. The reconstructions, moreover, provide us with evidence that phase D must have been a long one. Ħaġar Qim is also unique among the Maltese monuments in that globigerina limestone is used as the material of construction throughout, for the façade and outer wall, as well as for those of the chambers. The slabs used in the outer wall are often extremely large, and include the enormous globigerina slab already referred to at the beginning of this chapter as the largest single stone used in any of the temples.

The slabs forming the base of the façade are smaller, but they are beautifully dressed to a regular shape, as are the blocks which are laid in courses above them. The walls of the rooms in the interior are also, with two notable exceptions, constructed

Plate 12

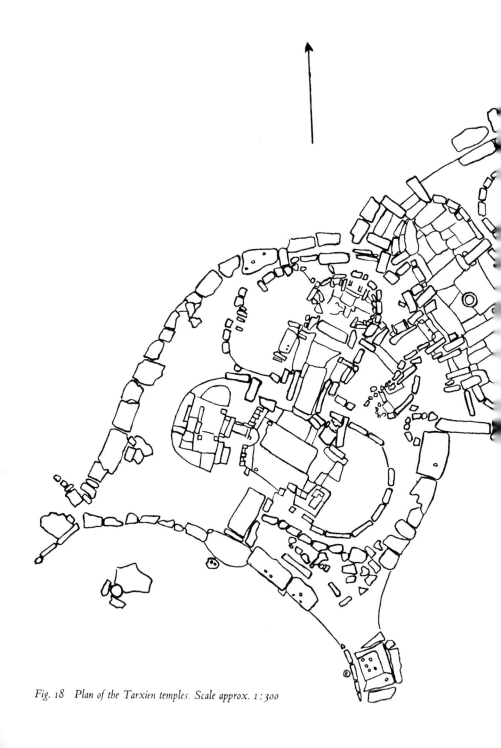

Fig. 18 Plan of the Tarxien temples. Scale approx. 1 : 300

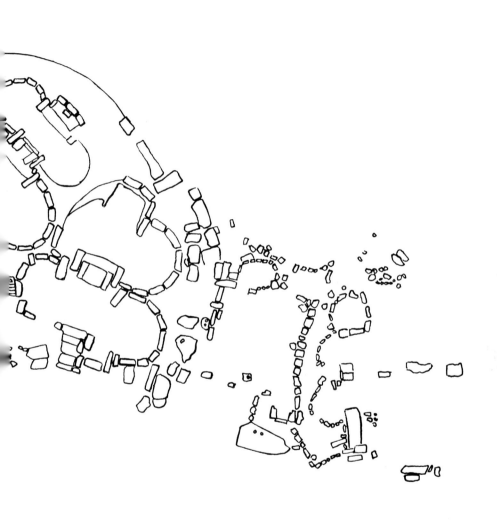

Plate 15

of slabs, more or less well dressed, above which one or more courses of rectangular blocks sometimes survive. These courses of blocks are corbelled inwards, so as to narrow the space to be roofed. The exceptions are the two semicircular chambers opening off the first court, immediately behind the façade. The walls of these chambers are composed of very rough blocks and irregular slabs of globigerina limestone assembled in a manner reminiscent of the technique used to build the inner walls of the Ġgantija. Accordingly it seems possible, as Mayr first suggested, that they are the oldest surviving part of the structure, and perhaps belong to an early part of phase D.

That globigerina limestone was not again used for the outer walls or façade of a temple, so far as we can tell, is not surprising. Normally, and rightly, the Maltese builders judged it to be too soft for this purpose. The outer wall of Ħaġar Qim has suffered very greatly from weathering, especially on the seaward side. When not reduced entirely to mere stumps, the huge stones that compose this side of the wall are gnarled and riddled with holes, and the fantastic shapes into which they have been worked by the salt wind in the course of ages add considerably to the romantic charm of the ruins at the present day. The somewhat less exposed façade has sustained the assaults of time rather better, and with the aid of some careful and judicious restoration we can still today get some idea of the effect that it was originally intended to make, especially if we take into account the evidence provided by some fragments of Fig. 19 what appears to have been a sort of 'architects' model' of such a façade found in the excavation of the Tarxien temples. The fallen blocks of the first two courses have been replaced, which could be done with absolute confidence, because of their position, and the evidence provided by the Tarxien model.

It may be that globigerina limestone was used at Ħaġar Qim simply because supplies of it were closer at hand than anything else, but it seems clear from the façade that for this at any rate it was deliberately chosen because its softness and consistency allowed a smooth and exact finish to be obtained. A new preoccupation with the production of regular stonework is evident also in most parts of the interior. It is as if the Maltese builders had suddenly fallen in love with the effect produced by highly finished masonry, and had resolved to enjoy it wherever possible. Of course, the unsightly walls of the older temples were probably not intended to be seen in all their nakedness. At the Ġgantija there is some direct evidence that the rugged chamber-walls were concealed by a thick coat of daub faced with a thinner layer of limestone plaster. Some fragments of the clay and plaster have survived in position on the walls; a specimen has been removed to the Museum. The surface of the plaster appears to have been painted with a bright red pigment, and paintings of the interior of the Ġgantija done soon after its excavation in 1827 show larger areas of painted plaster on the walls, so that we should perhaps imagine the walls of these inner chambers as entirely painted in blood-red. This receives some confirmation from the extensive traces of red paint on the walls of the Hypogeum. Be this as it may, there can be little doubt that the masonry of the inner walls of the later temples was intended to be seen just as it was; if they were painted, the paint must have been applied directly to the stone and all traces have disappeared. The effect of the best-preserved parts of the walls of these inner chambers is even today very satisfying.

We have seen that the technical problems of moving and erecting really large slabs of stone had already been solved at the time of the construction of the outer wall of the Ġgantija. The massive stones were probably moved on rollers consisting of roughly spherical balls of limestone, which have been found in considerable numbers on the sites of the later temples, particularly at Tarxien, and at the Hypogeum. The innovations at Ħaġar Qim are the careful dressing of the slabs and blocks and the use of regular corbelling or false vaulting in the courses of blocks. The rough dressing was probably done by much the same means as were used to excavate the soft rock when making tomb-chambers, as for instance at the Hypogeum, where evidence of the methods used remains in some parts (see below, p. 132); namely, stone mauls or mallets and picks of horn or antler tines. The final finish was probably laboriously obtained with small flint blades. Hard stone adzes could have been used for some of this, but they are so notoriously rare among the finds (in contrast to axe-amulets, which are abundant in the later phases) that this seems unlikely. It is noticeable that the forward edges of the coursed blocks are invariably made slightly convex, and this same peculiarity is often visible in the edges of upright slabs, or of the window-like openings cut in them. Apart from the façade, the coursed blocks are best preserved in the right-hand rear chamber of the more or less regular part of the building. Here the stones of the two surviving courses each overhang the stones below them, but have been carefully finished in such a way that no sharp step is visible.

Plate 15

The Haġar Qim buildings contain also a number of novelties in the way of fittings. These include several types of altars, and various niches, or recesses made of slabs, some of them containing a pillar and others without it. Certain of these, such as those in the small rooms described on p. 103, were additions made to the building in phase E, but others again may have been installed during the latter part of phase D, when additions and reconstructions were still being made to the fabric of the buildings themselves. The altars include two mushroom-shaped ones that have no parallels in any of the other temples, a very elaborate and beautiful one carved on each of its four faces with a design of a tall plant growing out of a tub or pot, which is also unique, and finally an altar of slabs into which was incorporated a slab carved in relief with a double spiral pattern. The first two of these types, as well as the pillar-niches,

Plate 16
Plate 79

Plate 78

can be closely paralleled among the paraphernalia of Minoan-Mycenean religion. There may be something in all this to suggest that the influence of Aegean civilization, which is so obvious in phase E, may have begun already towards the end of phase D. Indeed, we cannot but wonder if the sudden interest in carefully dressed masonry first displayed so notably at Ħaġar Qim, is not also in some way a direct result of the beginning of contact with the Aegean.

It now remains to consider briefly such buildings as can be attributed to the fifth and final phase of the early Maltese culture. Apart from a number of monuments of minor importance, there are two large and important complexes that can be attributed almost in their entirety to this period: those of Mnajdra and Tarxien. The ruins of the former lie only a few hundred yards distant from those of Ħaġar Qim, at the bottom of the hill on which the latter stand, and so they may be described first. The attractive setting of the Mnajdra ruins, in a hollow which opens out on its south-west side to give a view of the sea and, once again, of Filfla, lend a special charm to them. The fantastic shapes to which the stones of the outer casing have been wrought by weathering produce a sense of being literally among the 'wrecks of time' in a surrealistic landscape, an impression heightened by the proximity of the sea, and the rugged outlines of the limestone hills.

Fig. 1 (13)
Plate 17

Apart from the small trefoil mentioned earlier, there are two main buildings at Mnajdra, both consisting of more or less regular units of the later type, having two sets of lateral chambers and a small rear recess behind the second pair. They are entered from the same side although they do not have a common façade, and are set at an angle of 45° to each other. One of the buildings, the later, appears never to have had a monumental façade of the ordinary type. The 1954 excavations showed that the more elaborate of the two buildings, the one lying to the south-west of the other, was the earlier. This building appears to have undergone several reconstructions and alterations, and to have been always more important than the one that was later added to it, thus affording a striking parallel to the situation at the Ġgantija. We will take the older building first.

The first pair of chambers (which can here scarcely be separated from the central area, so that the whole forms one large oval room) is the most important. The walls are made of huge, but beautifully dressed slabs, fitted together with great care, and these are surmounted by regular courses of dressed blocks. No less than four courses of these are preserved at one point, which overhang each other in the same way as those at Ħaġar Qim, though they have not been dressed with such skill as completely to avoid the stepped appearance. From the right-hand part of this area some steps lead through a window-like opening in one of the wall-slabs into an irregular chamber situated between the back of the inner wall and that of the outer casing. In this room were some complicated installations consisting of niches of slabs, with and without pillars. One of these, on the right of the entrance, is partially screened by a carefully finished slab with a window-like opening cut in it, and is supported on an elaborately carved pillar.

The excavations of 1944 have shown that the front chambers of the south-west building were constructed early in phase E, but were re-floored with *torba* later in that phase. The rear rooms are more difficult to interpret. To begin with, the left-hand chamber has been completely deformed by being converted, probably in a relatively late reconstruction, into a series of three pillar-niches. A special entrance leading to these directly from the left-hand portion of the front room was also created at about the same time. This entrance is elaborately decorated and is one of the best-known features in any of the Maltese temples through having been so often reproduced. The ornament, which is applied not only to the doorway itself but also to the

Plates 18, 20, 22

Plate 20

Plate 19

flanking slabs, consists of rows of small regular hollows made with a drill (probably a bow-drill); this produced a very dignified and pleasing honeycomb effect. The right-hand chamber, on the other hand, is of little intrinsic interest. It is small and very roughly constructed, for which reason Mayr thought that it might be the earliest part of the building, but it proved impossible to check this, since the whole area had already been excavated down to bedrock. The rear recess is of the normal type, and contains the usual pillar niche of slabs.

The outer casing of this building consists of large undressed slabs and blocks of coralline limestone (globigerina being used exclusively for the interior). This had collapsed over much of its length, and has recently been replaced by the Museum authorities with a rubble wall. At a point on the north side of the outer wall, near where it adjoins that of the later building, are the remains of an entrance leading into a chamber between the inner and outer walls. From this chamber it is possible to look out, through a small but neatly cut rectangular opening in one of the wall-slabs, into the front room of the building. This arrangement recalls one in the rear right-hand chamber at Haġar Qim, only the hole in this case is oval in shape and gives on an area fenced off within the chamber by a wall of small slabs. A still closer parallel occurs in the Tarxien temples, and we shall defer any discussion of the significance of this feature until we come to describe the latter. The façade of the south-west building is relatively well preserved, but being made of coralline limestone, it has a rugged impressiveness more akin to that of the Ġgantija than to the elegance of the Haġar Qim façade.

Plate 22

The north-east building is much less imposing, though it is larger than the one just described. Since it lies further up the hill than the older building, the ground had to be levelled by making a platform of rough boulders. This platform was consolidated by means of a retaining wall which runs some distance in front of the entrance to the building, and seems to have taken the place of a monumental façade. This platform was investigated in 1954 by means of a small sounding beneath the floor of the building. This had been previously done by Ashby in order to ascertain the nature of the platform, but this time it was possible to show, by means of the broken pottery found among the stones of the construction, that it, and consequently the temple which rested on it, had been made no earlier than an advanced stage of phase E. The walls of the chambers of the north-east building are constructed in the usual way with upright slabs surmounted by courses of dressed blocks, but the stones used are consistently much smaller than those employed in the south-west temple. The slabs scarcely ever exceed 3 ft in height, and then only slightly. The work is competent enough, but without being too fanciful you can see that it exhibits a loss of the mastery displayed in the work of the south-west temple and at Ḥaġar Qim.

Plate 21

The front chambers have no features of interest, apart from the usual pair of altars, set one on each side of the passage leading to the rear chambers. On about the middle of the upright slab which serves to screen the left-hand altar and separate it from the corresponding chamber there is a small relief-carving; this represents, as far as can be made out, a small megalithic shrine, rather like the one represented in the model from Mġarr. The rear rooms are similar to the front ones in point of construction, and in the rear recess there is the usual box-like construction of slabs with its pillar. However, there are one or two features worthy of note. One of the wall-slabs of the right-hand chamber is pierced with a rough hole, which perhaps served the same purpose as that already noted in the south-west temple, though in this case there is no trace of a chamber to be seen. The most interesting feature, though, is a small room set behind the walls of the south-west chamber. It is entered through a window-like opening in a slab which is

Plate 76

Plate 77

itself enclosed in a trilithon. Inside this tiny chamber is a small niche composed of slabs with a central pillar. The outer wall of this building, which is for the most part relatively well preserved, is composed, like the walls of the inner chambers, of stones much inferior in size to those used in that of the south-west building.

The entrance to the north-east building is very unusual; in fact, as it survives at present, there appear to be two doorways side by side. The right-hand one, however, is slightly off-centre and may, like those flanking the passage to the rear rooms, originally have been an altar. The other is central, and most unusual in construction, Two uprights (now largely destroyed) formed a short corridor leading up to a large window-like opening cut in a massive slab which blocks the passage. The top half of this slab has been destroyed, but there is no reason to doubt that the opening was originally in a single slab. This is the only time that this device is used for an entrance other than that to a small niche or chamber.

Though the Mnajdra ruins are of the greatest interest, the most complete picture of the fifth phase of the Maltese culture is undoubtedly to be obtained from the Tarxien temples. Apart from the small east building already mentioned above, and a few rather scattered remains near it, three separate buildings can be distinguished in the Tarxien complex, which all intercommunicate. That these were built at different times and joined together in a rather *ad hoc* manner was obvious from the first. Zammit thought that the easternmost of the three was built first, the middle one coming next, and the westernmost last; this has proved to be basically correct, though the excavations carried out there in 1954 demonstrated that the full story was somewhat more complicated than this simple scheme would suggest.

Despite the evidence about order of construction, however, it will be convenient to describe the buildings beginning with

Fig. 1 (12)
Fig. 18

the westernmost or latest portion, since it is through this that the monument is entered at the present day. A discussion of the chronology can be left until later. Of all the Tarxien monu/ ments the western temple has suffered the most from the ravages of time and agriculture, and so is liable to disappoint from the architectural point of view anyone who comes to it after having

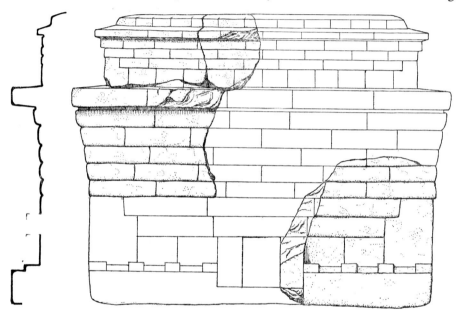

Fig. 19   Reconstruction of a limestone model of the façade of a temple of the later type from the fragments found in the Tarxien temples. Height of right-hand fragment 6¾ in.

just inspected the remains of Haġar Qim and Mnajdra, though it more than makes up for this by the splendour of the carved ornament it contains. The entrance is set at the centre of a large, deeply curved façade, which is now miserably ruined, though its general line is still traceable. At either end of this is a curious feature consisting of a horizontal slab with several conical holes drilled vertically through it. Enough

Figs. 18, 20

remains to show that these slabs were originally enclosed in a kind of niche or recess of slabs. Zammit suggested that these slabs were intended for a kind of ritual game played with certain of the smaller of the limestone balls; of these some were found nearby, and as we have seen, they were probably used as rollers for moving stones. Though we cannot hope to prove with any

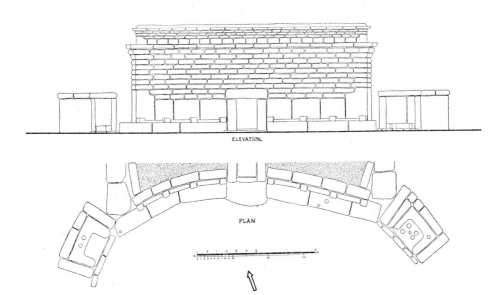

ELEVATION

PLAN

Fig. 20 Conjectural reconstruction of the façade of the Tarxien temples, utilizing the evidence of the surviving portions of late façades and of the model, Fig. 19. Height 30 ft, span 110 ft

certainty what was the original intention of these installations, I shall suggest what seems to me a more probable one at the appropriate time.

Passing through the short corridor which forms the entrance, we come to a paved court, with a pair of the usual semicircular chambers opening off it to right and left respectively. There is a shallow hollow in the paving at the centre of the court, where

Plates 23, 24

the stones are much cracked and show signs of heavy burning. Around this court was grouped the richest collection of carved ornament to be found on any site in the Maltese islands. The carving is done in relatively high relief on the faces of a number of blocks of stone, and the patterns are all to some extent based on the spiral, though some represent very fanciful interpretations of it. Most of the decorated stones form part of two miniature façades, which imitate the form of the monumental façades in front of temples, and serve here to separate the sidechambers from the central court. The lefthand one has even an entrance passage formed of upright slabs, on two of which

Plate 23, centre

Mrs D. Woolner has recently observed and studied some remarkable *graffiti* of ships. It seems most unlikely that these are actually of the same age as the temples, but they are nevertheless of the greatest interest, since they may have been executed not long after the templeculture came to an end.

Spiral patterns are also carved on the two altars; these, as usual, flank the entrance to the rear chambers, but are rather more elaborate than usual. The righthand one is hollow, and is surmounted by a small slab with a windowlike opening carved in it; it is surrounded by a miniature trilithon. The charred bones of animal sacrifices were tossed through this windowslab into the hollow interior of the altar, which was found to be full of them. In the carved front of the altar is a lunate opening, which the original excavator found blocked with a wellfitting stone plug. On removing this, the sharp flint blade of the sacrificial knife was found lying inside, where it had been neatly replaced after use. Thus we have conclusive proof that the sacrifice of animal offerings was a part of Maltese religion, at any rate in the period of the later temples. The bones were those of sheep, goats, pigs and cattle, and carvings of all these animals were found in the temples. A ram, a pig

Fig. 23
Fig. 25

and some goats appear carved on a block which lies at the back of the front lefthand chamber, and carvings of a sow and some cattle found elsewhere will be mentioned again when we arrive at that part of the buildings.

Finally, to end the catalogue of the contents of this remarkable area, mention must be made of the remains of the base and lower right-hand portion of the body of what must originally have been a colossal statue of the Maltese fertility deity. Quarrying of the stone, which may have been carried on in relatively recent times, had reduced the remains to a mere 3 ft in height, but there can be no doubt that the original must have stood at least 8 ft high. A comparison with some of the statuettes recovered during the excavations at the Tarxien temples would seem to indicate that the figure was probably seated. It is quite unique in being the only piece of monumental sculpture belonging to such an early period known in the Western Mediterranean (the Aegean included). Not until several hundred years later was anything attempted on a comparable scale, even in Greece.

The rear rooms of the first building are reached through the usual short passage. The remains here are somewhat confused, and it is difficult to see in them anything closely approximating to the usual layout. The back recess occurs in a very much elaborated form, the small niche being set on a raised platform, the front of which is formed by a long slab of stone, whose surface is carved with two rows of rather elaborate running spirals. It is the largest of the carved stones found in the Maltese temples. The place of the left-hand chamber is taken by what may have been an irregular open area bounded by a wall of small slabs, whilst the right-hand chamber is replaced by a number of small irregular rooms and spaces. The stones in this latter area all show signs of heavy burning on their upper parts, for this part of the temples was utilized for a cremation cemetery by the people who came to inhabit the Maltese islands immediately after the temple-culture came to an end.

From the north-east corner of this area a corridor leads into

Plate 25

the middle temple. This building is unique among the Maltese buildings in that it consists of no less than three pairs of lateral chambers opening off courts, which diminish progressively in size towards the back. A possible explanation of how this came about is offered below (pp. 123–4) in the section dealing with the chronology of the temples.

The first pair, along with the central area, form a sort of open oval area paved with huge slabs and of noble proportions. A circular stone hearth, much discoloured by fire, occupies a central position in this area. The walls, which are composed of large slabs surmounted by courses of blocks, are also heavily discoloured by a fire; this fire seems to have been connected with an earlier floor than the present pavement, since the latter shows no trace of burning, while the walls even below the level of the pavement are affected. Two small irregular rooms open off the southern side of this area. The left-hand one contains some niches made of stone slabs, whose surfaces are heavily burnt, whilst one wall of the right-hand chamber is composed of large slabs on which have been carved in relief the figures of two bulls, and a sow suckling a litter of thirteen piglets. The bulls are of the humped or Indian type, like those shown on the potsherd from Tarxien mentioned above.

Fig. 25

The usual flanking altars in the passage to the next room are present, but are here set in front of the projecting upright slabs that normally separate them from the lateral chambers. This was necessitated by the huge threshold slab which forms a step about a foot in height and which extends beyond the width of the corridor as far as these screens, thus filling the space usually occupied by the altars. The fragments of a huge stone bowl were found standing on the left-hand portion of this slab, which has been reconstructed and now stands in the adjoining chamber.

The passage leading to the second set of chambers is blocked to a certain height by a rectangular slab of stone carved with

Plate 26

a pattern of two spirals with a triangle between. It has a close parallel in the slab from Hagar Qim which has the same pattern more roughly executed, though it occupied a different position, apparently. Almost certainly the pattern is intended as a stylized representation of eyes, conceived of as guarding the place behind. Closely similar ones occur on two slabs which were used to close contemporary rock-cut tombs in Sicily, though in that case a very stylized representation of the rest of the figure is added, making the interpretation more certain. The reason why these prophylactic eyes were placed just there can of course only be guessed at, but a possible explanation will be suggested later when the chronology of the buildings is discussed (pp. 122–3).

The chambers whither this blocked passage leads, are much smaller than the outer ones, and only remarkable in that each is partially shut off from the central area (which once more has a circular stone hearth in the middle) by a remarkably finely carved stone screen. Each one has a symmetrical pattern composed of four spirals arranged in a double oculus pattern. The third set of chambers is smaller still, and lacks the carved screens of the second, though it contains some small niches made of slabs. At the back of the central space is the customary recess containing a niche of slabs with the usual central pillar. Both these sets of rooms are extremely well constructed of slabs and dressed blocks, and are floored with *torba*, not paved like the first. In the left-hand room of the rear pair a single block survives on top of one of the wall-slabs which has been choked up at the back with small stones so that the upper surface is at an angle to the horizontal. This has been claimed as evidence that the room was covered by a true dome. Were this so, it would be the earliest appearance of this architectural feature. But the evidence is very slight; besides, the raising of the back of this stone may have been quite recent, as part of some unfinished attempt to remove and re-utilize it.

Plate 28

To reach the third temple, it is necessary to return to the first pair of chambers of the middle temple. An opening in the wall at the south-east end of the right-hand one of these—once a regularly constructed doorway, though now only one side survives—leads into it. In approaching this exit you pass a point where one of the huge paving slabs has been removed (by Ashby), revealing both their great thickness and the fact that some of the stone rollers used to manœuvre them into position have been left in place under them. Just beyond the exit, on the left-hand side, is a narrow stone staircase of steps leading up behind the chamber wall to what must originally have been a passage between the chamber walls of the middle and easternmost temples. Traces of the *torba* flooring of this passage are still visible near the top of the staircase.

The third, or eastern temple presents at present a very unusual aspect. It is a building of the normal later type with two sets of chambers, but the left-hand ones of each pair are both strangely deformed, apparently because of the proximity of the corresponding right-hand chambers of the middle temple. The walls of this part of the building had been completely destroyed over much of their length at the time of excavation but enough remained to show that they were built of unusually small slabs. Zammit later reconstructed the destroyed portions with material found nearby. The corridors and the right-hand chambers of the building were, on the contrary, built with more than usually massive slabs, being some of the largest to be found anywhere in the complex, and in the chambers they are surmounted by unusually long and massive blocks. The rear recess is exceptionally large and massive for a temple of the later phase—indeed, much more like that of the south building at Ġgantija.

In the rear right-hand chamber of this building a rectangular opening, similar to that in the south-west building at Mnajdra, has been cut out between two of the wall-slabs. This is now enlarged and distorted by the effects of weathering, but was originally neatly worked. Behind the wall at this point is a chamber, as at Mnajdra, in the thickness between the inner and outer walls of the building, which is entered through a short corridor from a door in the outer wall, still visible, though very much weathered. In addition to the rectangular opening, a hole has been made in one of the slabs; this forms an additional communication between the small chamber in the walls and the main one of the temple. It is in the form of a tube, which enters the stone at knee height in the small closet, to emerge almost at ground level in the chamber. The most obvious explanation for these phenomena are that they are arrangements to facilitate the practice of some sort of 'priestcraft', which may have included oracular pronouncements and the mysterious appearance of a sign or talisman at the foot of the worshipper.

Having completed the straightforward description of the remains as they stand, it is now necessary to say a little about the order of construction of the various parts, as it appears from the latest investigations. Zammit, basing himself chiefly on the evidence of a development in style he believed to be discernible in the architecture and the technique of the carved ornament, thought that the three temples were built in the reverse order to that in which they have been described here. The temple last described was taken to be the earliest, since it possessed no carved ornament, and was constructed, at least on the best-preserved side, from large, but beautifully dressed and fitted slabs, like those used in the main rooms of the south-west temple at Mnajdra. Furthermore, the deformed left-hand chambers seemed to provide clear evidence that the building had been altered at the time of the building of the middle temple, which must therefore have been later. This piece of evidence, once apparently the soundest of all, has not been confirmed by the recent excavations, though these have shown that the eastern temple is indeed older than the present middle one.

Plate 27

The eastern and middle temples at Tarxien have the peculiarity of being in some sense rock-cut monuments, in that the floors of most of the chambers have been sunk below the natural level of the rock, which has been excavated to a certain depth varying from chamber to chamber. The purpose of this is the more obscure, in that they were subsequently raised again, by successive re-floorings with earth and *torba,* to about the natural level. This peculiar practice was not confined to Tarxien, but has been found also at Ħaġar Qim, and to a lesser extent at Mnajdra and the Ġgantija.

Plate 27

The floor of the right-hand rear room of the eastern temple is thus about 3 ft below the natural level of the rock. Above it are two superimposed *torba* floors, beneath the lower of which were found fragments of pottery belonging to an early stage of phase E, thus proving the building to be approximately contemporary with the south-east temple at Mnajdra. In the left-hand chambers, however, no hollowing-out of the bedrock had taken place. More surprising results were obtained from excavations in the two inner sets of chambers of the middle temple. Here trenches were cut below the floor levels of the two left-hand chambers (since the right-hand ones had already been emptied in the course of earlier investigations), and revealed once more two floor levels, below the second of which the fragments of pottery all belonged to phase D.

A temple, therefore, stood on this site before the erection of the east building, but it was not the present one, as was proved by the finding of potsherds of phase E type beneath one of the wall-slabs of the rear left-hand chamber. The structure must have been rebuilt, following the old plan, in phase E and, if the style of the potsherds means anything, at a relatively advanced stage of this phase.

Besides illustrating the chronological relations between the eastern and middle temples, this discovery may throw light on some other matters. It may, for instance, suggest the reason

for the slab with the oculus-spirals which bars access to these Plate 26
rooms from the outer court. It may be that, standing as they do
on the site of the oldest shrine (if we except the small east
building) in the complex, they were considered as exceptionally
sacred, and not to be entered by the profane, but only by the
priests, who may perhaps have reached them by means of the
enigmatic steps and the *torba*-floored corridor between the walls.

The exact chronological relation between the present middle
temple and the western one is difficult to determine with
certainty. Zammit's stylistic arguments carry considerable
weight here. The middle temple, though the stones used in its
construction are, with the exception of those employed in the
outer rooms, smaller than those employed for the eastern
temple, is nevertheless comparable with the latter in the excellent
workmanship displayed, and is much superior in this respect
to the west building, where the building technique seems
definitely decadent. The conclusion that it is earlier than the
latter is supported in a different way by the contrasting styles
displayed in the carved ornament in the two buildings. The
carved slab that blocks the passage to the inner recesses of the
middle temple, and the carved screens that stand in the rooms Plate 28
immediately behind it bear combinations of plain spirals. The
background, in the case of the screens, is filled up with drilled
decoration, and the raised surface of the spirals is flat. Contrasting with this restrained, 'classical', style is the 'baroque'
profusion of branched spirals and wild irregular derivatives of Plates 23-5
the spiral carved on the blocks in the western temple. No
drilling is used, and the surface of the raised designs is normally
convex.

Both these points tell in favour of the western temple having
been erected after the middle one. Excavation confirms this to
the extent of showing that there was only one floor level in the
former, and the pottery found beneath it all belongs to an
advanced stage of phase E. On the other hand, the middle

temple, with its three sets of chambers, represents the most advanced type of plan. The outer set was certainly added when the rest was reconstructed in phase E, since only late pottery has been found beneath the paving slabs, which rest almost directly on the rock—here but slightly hollowed out. Perhaps this outer court was meant to be used for the public part of the worship when the rest of the building was segregated for the use of the initiated. Again, it seems partly intended as a device for linking up the middle and the western temples. So then, although it seems for several reasons likely that the middle temple was reconstructed before the western one was built, there is at present no completely uncontrovertible proof of this.

Two general conclusions seem to follow from this short analysis of the evidence concerning the chronological succession of the buildings at Tarxien. First, the idea, already suggested by the buildings at Mnajdra, of a certain decline in architectural skill towards the end of phase E from an apogee early in that phase, is confirmed. The second is that the middle temple at Tarxien does not really represent a final typological development of the standard temple-unit. The addition of the third pair of chambers was not, that is, dictated by a development of the ritual, but was made necessary by the sequestration of the inner pairs for special uses, or by the desire to link up with the western temple, or both. Thus it is, in fact, an aberrant type.

Several other minor temples date apparently from phase E.
Fig. 1 (15, 16) The two best-known of these are Buġibba and Tal Qadi, both of which are badly damaged. Tal Qadi consists of a single unit of the later type, the outline of the two sets of chambers and small rear recess being quite clear, though the stones have been robbed to the foundations. Lack of complete excavation and the fact that a later wall has been built across part of it obscure the plan at Buġibba, but the façade and two front chambers survive, and it seems likely that it was a unit of the normal later type. The Buġibba temple, lying as it does close to

the shore on the peninsula which marks the eastern limit of
St Paul's Bay, is most pleasantly situated. Appropriately enough,
being the closest to the sea of all the Maltese temples, this one
yielded the only carving representing fish so far in Malta. A
further very tiny shrine, Xrobb il-Għaġin, which now hangs
perilously over the edge of the cliffs on the south-east coast of
Malta, has also the later form, but it has produced a slab
decorated with drilled decoration, and probably dates from
phase D. Yet another smallish late temple at Ħal Ġinwi, seems
to have had the peculiarity of having rooms that were squarish *Fig. 1 (17)*
in plan instead of semicircular. Finally there is Borġ in-Nadur, *Fig. 1 (25)*
where the building seems to have consisted of a large oval court
bounded by a megalithic wall, in the south-west corner of
which is the entrance to a small monument of the later type.

Having now surveyed the general development of the
Maltese temples and described the chief examples, I shall con-
clude the discussion of them with a few remarks on one or two
general aspects and problems. It is evident from the preceding
pages that the larger temple-complexes of Malta grew up rather
in the way that the medieval cathedrals of Europe generally did.
They were not planned and built as a whole, but were altered,
added to, or re-built wholly or in part over a period spanning
many generations. Neither the individual units, nor the complexes as a whole appear to have any consistent orientation,
though mostly the entrances face in some direction between
south-east and south-west. Exceptions could be found even to
this, however, so that it seems that orientation was not important.
There is no sign of any special interest in any of the heavenly
bodies. Some of the monuments command excellent views, but
again this does not seem to be essential. Interest is concentrated
rather on the interior than the exterior.

As we have seen, the building techniques used made great
strides as the development proceeded. In the early stages, rough
boulders, small at first, then progressively larger, were used for

the making of both the inner and outer walls, though pillars and rough slabs were already in use for corridors and portals, and for paving slabs and steps. The buildings produced became larger and larger, and this style of building culminated in the Ġgantija, whose outer wall, however, with its huge slabs of coralline limestone, heralds a new and more refined style of construction. With the same phase Haġar Qim shows the revolution in building technique completed, constructed as it is entirely of dressed slabs and blocks of globigerina limestone. The enthusiasm for accurately dressed masonry, which runs riot at Haġar Qim, was later tempered by practical considerations of durability insofar as the outer casing is concerned, leading to a reversion to the more intractable coralline limestone for this; but all the late temples make use of dressed slabs and blocks of globigerina for their inner walls and decorative panels.

One very vexed question is that of whether, and, if so, how the temples were roofed. Very various opinions have been, and still are, entertained about this. The grandiose, but rather specious, reconstructions published by the Italian architect Carlo Ceschi just before the last war, have tended rather to discredit the idea that they were roofed, but I am rather of the opinion that they must have been, though in a more modest manner than that imagined by Ceschi, no doubt. Several arguments seem to me to point in this direction. Firstly, whenever the rubble walls of the earlier temples are preserved to a sufficient height they show a marked overhang, which suggests the beginning of vaulting. This is visible at Mġarr, but is most marked in the large rear chamber of the Ġgantija, where the walls are preserved to a height of almost 17 ft. The corbelling, or false-vaulting, a technique employed in the later temples, has already been mentioned. It seems unlikely that the walls would have been constructed in this way if the roofing at any rate of the semicircular rooms had not been intended.

The next question is, what form did the roofing take and

Plates 4, 9

what materials were employed? A completely domed structure seems unlikely for a number of reasons. It seems highly improbable that such a structure could have been made using the technique employed in building the earlier temples. Nor does it seem possible that the corbelled blocks of the later buildings can have been carried up to form a full half-dome over the semicircular chambers. The true corbelled vault is circular in plan and is given solidity by the mutual pressure of its component parts on each other. In place of this, the semi-circular course of corbelled blocks in the Maltese temples has to be held at each end by a tall pillar-like slab, which, however, was only high enough to serve four or five courses of blocks. Above this level the roof, if it existed, must have been flat.

Plates 20, 22, 28

Some confirmation is given to this conclusion by one or two models representing apparently megalithic shrines that have been found on various sites. From Mġarr comes a tiny lime-stone model representing a small building in plan resembling the smallest one at Mġarr itself, but apparently made of slabs. The roofing appears to have been done partly by courses of corbelled blocks, but completed by a series of horizontal slabs. Similar roofing arrangements seem to be indicated in the small shrine carved in relief above one of the altars of the later building at Mnajdra, and on a tiny amulet of greenstone in the form of a shrine found at Tarxien. Finally, this is exactly the form of roofing which is imitated at full size in the skeuo-morphic carving of some of the inner halls of the rock-cut monument of Hal Saflieni.

Plate 77

Plate 76
Fig. 27

An exactly similar form of roofing is used today in some of the Maltese farmhouses, but it is only feasible for rooms of strictly limited breadth. About 8 ft is the maximum span which can be covered by a slab of Maltese limestone without introducing central supports. Most of the rooms in the later Maltese temples have spans far greater than this, even when reduced by several courses of corbelling, and there is no trace that any central pillars or other supports ever existed in the rooms. Thus, while a few of the early and some of the minor later temples could have been roofed with stone, this is clearly out of the question for most of the main monuments. If they were roofed, some other material must have been used. Personally, I am inclined to think that it was done with wood. Suitable wood is now scarce in the Maltese islands, and where it does occur it is in artificial gardens or plantations, and carefully tended. Yet in prehistoric Malta there may well have been a sufficient supply on hand, even if the alleged tree represented on the sherd from Tarxien along with two humped bulls is not a tree at all.

One feature of the Tarxien temples could be interpreted as positive evidence in favour of wooden roofs. This is the signs of intense burning visible on the walls of the middle temple at Tarxien. The conflagration that caused them evidently happened while the temple was still in use, since they go below the present floor level. What was there in the temples to burn so furiously—unless they were roofed with wood? One further piece of circumstantial evidence in favour of the temples having been roofed may be added here. The elaborately carved patterns on slabs and blocks of globigerina limestone which are so frequent a feature in the later temples were mostly in good condition and very fresh when found. Yet in the Tarxien temples, where the originals were covered after excavation by copies made in the same stone, the latter have weathered badly in some cases after being exposed to the elements for less than 30 years. It seem unlikely that delicate carvings, which must have been very precious, would be left in such danger, and their condition when found also argues against this. This point, by the way, if valid, implies that the central spaces as well as the semicircular rooms must have been roofed, since more carvings have been found in these than in the rooms themselves.

Before concluding this chapter on the monuments it will

be necessary to cast a quick glance at the line of development taken by the rock-cut tombs after the built monuments had definitely separated themselves off as places of worship. In the former, progress seems to be neither so universal nor so unilineal as in the case of the temples. The simple chamber-tomb con- sisting of a single oval- or kidney-shaped vault entered from a pit, which was already being built in phase B, as the Xemxija tombs show, continued to be used and made throughout the whole period. Even natural caves, whose use perhaps goes back to phase A, continued to be employed as burial places, a late example being the cave or fissure at Bur Mgħez which was in use in phases D and E. Apart from the group at Xemxija, the only simple chamber-tomb that has survived undamaged is a very small one discovered at Nadur; this belongs to phase D, according to the pottery found in it. There are, however, a few other tombs which, when found, consisted simply of shallow depressions in the rock, but may well originally have been chamber-tombs, whose upper parts have been removed through the subsequent quarrying of the rock. Of this type is a single tomb found at Busbisija, belonging to phase D, and the group of five at Żebbuġ, belonging to phase C, which have already been discussed in Ch. II. A tomb with a bell-shaped chamber entered from the top is reported to have been found near Buqana, but it has been destroyed. The pottery belongs to phases C and D. Tombs of this shape are common in Period II, but this is the only one so far reported which dates from Period I.

The Hypogeum of Ħal Saflieni is at present the sole example of a rock-cut monument with a more complex ground plan, and it is at the opposite extreme in point of size and complexity from the simple chambers that we have been discussing. Basically this amazing monument is an aggregate of many small rock-cut chambers, each one corresponding to a single tomb of the simple type, linked together by a series of underground halls, passages and stairways. The germ of this

Fig. 1 (27)
Figs. 14, 15
Plate 32

Fig. 1 (7), (6)
Fig. 16

Fig. 1 (10)

Fig. 15
Plates 32, 33

development can perhaps be seen in tombs 1 and 2 at Xemxija, whose chambers are linked by a short underground passage, though each retains its separate entrance of the normal pit type. From such insignificant beginnings the vast Hypogeum may have arisen. Certainly this great catacomb was not made all at once, or to a preconceived plan, any more than were the temples. On the evidence of the pottery found in it, the excavation of these labyrinthine precincts must have been carried on intermittently over several centuries.

The rock-cut chambers comprising the Hypogeum are cut into the top of a natural hill. They extend over an area of roughly 1600 sq. ft, and are laid out on three levels or storeys. The third and lowest of these reaches a depth of about 30 ft below the surface of the rock. It is impossible here to give a full description of this complicated labyrinth, so only some general indications will be attempted of the character of the chambers and halls on each level.

The original entrance to the monument has been considerably damaged by the building of houses above it (see Ch. 1, p. 22), the foundation walls of which criss-cross some of the chambers of the first storey so as greatly to hinder the visitor from obtaining any clear impression of the layout of this level. It would seem that there was some sort of megalithic building before the entrance at one time, since unmistakable remains of it were found when a road was being made in front of the new houses in 1909. The entrance to the Hypogeum is through a built trilithon which leads directly to the first level. All the chambers on this level are irregular in shape and relatively roughly finished, with the exception of a large and very deep one known as the 'well'; this was probably constructed later, at the same time as the elaborate inner halls, with which it has some features in common. The rest of the chambers on the first level probably date from phases B and C, and the innermost of them, which are rather better finished, from phase D.

Apart from the complexity of the plan, there is little to surprise about the first level. It is only when the second level is reached that a change becomes manifest. The halls become larger, and both halls and chambers are better finished, but these are not the only, nor the most remarkable, innovations. More interesting are the purely decorative features that appear. Megalithic slabs had already been employed in the upper storey, as we have seen, but in these inner rooms the living rock is often elaborately carved to represent megalithic masonry of the type found in the temples of phases D and E. One hall in particular has an elaborate version of a megalithic façade carved at one end with courses of corbelled blocks above. Several small chambers open off the other sides of this room, and each one is provided with an imitation trilithon entrance. Passing through the door in the centre of the imitation façade (or through a broken portion on the left-hand side) we enter another chamber, which is smaller, but no less elaborately carved. The wall on the left is occupied by a beautifully carved imitation façade, above which are once more carvings represent-ing courses of corbelled blocks. Behind this façade is a small chamber, kidney-shaped in plan; this was also carefully finished and elaborately carved, though it has either been subsequently damaged, or else it was undergoing some kind of alteration and enlargement when the building was finally abandoned. It is popularly known as the 'Holy of Holies', and the name is justified insofar as the room seems to have fulfilled a ritual function as well as being used for burial.

Other halls on the second level of the Hypogeum, though not embellished with carvings, are decorated with painted patterns, mostly on the ceiling. One has on its ceiling a pattern of loose running spirals, and another is covered with a sort of honeycomb pattern of Archimedes spirals, each enclosed in a hexagon. All these patterns are executed in red paint, and traces of red paint can also be found in the large hall mentioned above,

Plate 29

Plate 30

Plate 31

principally on the façade, which may have been entirely painted in red. On one of the other walls of this hall are traces of a chequer-board pattern painted in black and white, but this is the only vestige of painting in any other colour than red. The rooms of the second and third level show many traces of red paint on the walls and ceilings in dots, lines or solid panels.

The rooms of the third storey are reached by means of a staircase through an elaborately carved doorway in the wall on the right of the entrance to the antechamber of the 'Holy of Holies'. The seven upper steps are ancient, but the lowest one and the 'catwalk' which permits the visitor to explore these chambers despite the high partitions of rock that separate them, are modern additions. The chambers of this lowest level are narrow and high. In this they resemble the 'well' near the entrance, already mentioned. Another common feature is the presence of pilasters of rock which jut out of the walls at intervals. It seems very likely that in fact the 'well' was excavated, in its present form, at any rate, in this last period of construction. At the end of this series of chambers comes a final one off which open four small oven-like chambers; these were obviously intended to be used for burials, but were found empty when the building was first explored.

The whole of this vast underground labyrinth was excavated in the soft rock (globigerina limestone) by means of wedges or picks of horn or antler. These were first driven into the rock with the aid of stone mallets (two of which were found in the Hypogeum), of which pieces, thus weakened, were then split away. When the desired dimensions had been attained, the walls of the chamber were smoothed with small flint implements, or, less probably, with small adzes. In some places where for some reason the finishing process has not taken place, the holes made by the picks can be clearly seen. Technically, one of the most interesting features is the way in which the numerous natural faults in the rock, which tend to run more or less vertically or horizontally, are frequently exploited to form a naturally smooth floor or wall for a chamber, without the necessity of applying the usual laborious finishing process. But the most astonishing thing of all, perhaps is the imitations of megalithic architecture so far underground. In the inner halls of Hal Saflieni it seems that we have come full circle; if the temples themselves originally began in the imitation of rock-tombs, here we have the most elaborate of the rock-tombs consciously imitating the temples.

It is, I hope, abundantly clear from the foregoing sketch of their development that the Maltese temples and tombs were something indigenous, rooted in the beliefs and customs of the people whose religion they express, and they evolved step by step with these. There seems no question of their having been introduced as a result of influence from other cultures. Never-theless, since it is possible to point out parallels abroad (though never exact ones), I shall devote a few lines here to one or two of the most significant of these.

Rock-tombs of the Xemxija type have many parallels in different areas, particularly in Italy and Sicily (they are known to Italian archaeologists as 'a forno' tombs when entered from a pit). But the use of simple rock-tombs is so widespread that general parallels have little meaning. Of greater interest are parallels with the Hypogeum. Some rock-tombs elsewhere do give signs of developing in a similarly labyrinthine fashion. The best parallels are afforded by some of the tombs in the Anghelu Ruju Cemetery in Sardinia, though none really attains anything like the complexity of Hal Saflieni, while the shape of the chambers is generally more or less rectangular. One at least of these tombs, however, has an internal façade, leading from one room to another, though it is much smaller and simpler than the Maltese examples.

The Maltese temples resemble some types of megalithic tomb not merely in methods of construction, but also in having chambers arranged in pairs symmetrically on either side of a passage, though admittedly the parallels are in North-West Europe rather than in the Mediterranean. A more significant feature, though, is the monumental façade, first introduced in the later Mġarr monument, which is concave in plan and delimits a crescentic area in front of the temple. At the Ġgantija it is clear that the façade was continued in the form of a megalithic wall round the circular platform, thus forming a *temenos,* or sacred enclosure in front of the temples, and there is some evidence that this may have been so at some other monuments also.

The forecourt area, devoted to rites connected with the dead, is a common feature of both rock-cut and megalithic tombs elsewhere. It is found in front of rock-cut and megalithic tombs in the Balearic islands and Sicily (where two tombs of the Castelluccio culture have quite elaborately carved concave façades), in tholos tombs in Spain, and widely in the megalithic tombs of North-West Europe. In ordinary megalithic tombs this area is necessary, since it is the only place where rites can be performed, the rest of the tomb being shut up; but in the Maltese monuments, where the whole building is devoted to cult purposes, it seems less necessary except for architectural effect, and it does not occur in front of the rock-tombs. Perhaps, then, we really have here a trait which the Maltese came to know in the course of those trading contacts that seem to have been such a feature of the life of the early island and coastal cultures of the Mediterranean basin, and which they took over and adapted to their own purposes.

CHAPTER IV

Religion and Life in Ancient Malta

SINCE ALMOST ALL the material we have of the first Maltese culture comes either from their temples or their tombs, it is naturally their religious life which we know most about; so it will be appropriate to say something on this aspect first. The ancient Maltese, as we have seen, buried their dead collectively, in rock-cut tombs, and with them placed food offerings, pots and other grave-goods, presumably to accompany them to a future life. The human bones found in these graves are always in complete disorder, and are mixed up with fragments of the pots—which are almost always broken— animal bones, and so on. This state of affairs can mean one of two things. Either the bodies were first allowed to rot elsewhere, and then later gathered up and buried as mere bags of bones, or else they were buried immediately in the tombs, perhaps in earth specially put there for this purpose, and were only later disturbed and jumbled by the introduction of fresh burials. Since we have no evidence of the places where the bodies might have been first put, and since a few complete skeletons have been found (at the Hypogeum), presumably of the last persons buried, I am inclined to believe that the second alternative represents the fact. The bodies, or the soil in which they were laid, were invariably impregnated with red ochre—quite a common feature of primitive burials. The ochre, which is more or less blood-colour, represents the blood, which is the life. That this is no far-fetched fancy we can see from what happened when a partially waterlogged well-tomb of this period was accidentally discovered in road-making, and the workmen reported that the bones were lying in 'fresh blood' (the dissolved red ochre)!

The first colonizers of Malta probably brought with them from Sicily some sort of simple ancestor cult, which in the quiet Maltese islands, cut off from the outer world, they began slowly to elaborate, building for themselves special stone sanctuaries to house its growing rites. Though we cannot say definitely that the earliest of these were not built originally as tombs themselves, we do know that they soon ceased to be so, and that all the more developed monuments were built specially as temples of the cult. The nature of the rites in the earlier stages we cannot hope to know; we only guess dimly that they took the form of some kind of propitiation of the spirits of the dead, and, with less assurance, that perhaps already the vague form of the spirit or goddess of fertility hovered over and permeated them. Is she perhaps bodied forth in that crude stone head found in tomb 5 at Żebbuġ? Or in those ghostly, evanescent suggestions of human, or super-human, shapes on the pottery of the same phase? We cannot say, and in all probability never shall be able to say for certain.

Plate 48

Figs. 4b, 5b

It is not until we reach the temples of phases D and E that we have somewhat clearer evidence to go on. One feature very much in evidence in these structures are the so-called rope-holes, V- or U-shaped holes with two mouths, which are found in abundance in the stones of these later temples. Some of these evidently had a plain practical purpose sufficiently indicated by their name. Their positions, in the jambs of doorways, etc., show that they were intended to hold the hinges or fastenings, probably of leather, of doors or screens. Other, larger holes (simple ones this time), which often occur in pairs, one on each side of a passage, are equally obviously intended to hold large wooden bars. But not all of the rope-holes can be explained in this way. Some have, indeed, though more doubtfully, been interpreted as holes for ropes used in dragging the stones to the temple where they were needed, but there remain others to which even this function cannot be

Plates 7, 8, 14

ascribed. These occur on horizontal surfaces, often in paving slabs, and their openings are often filled with carefully cut stone plugs. Examples of enormous size are to be seen just in front of the main entrances to the Haġar Qim, Mnajdra and Tarxien temples. These surely have a ritual significance! This suppo- sition is confirmed by the fact that some, when unplugged, were found to contain animal bones. The best example of this comes not from a temple, but from the Hypogeum, where a fine rope-hole, cut in the floor just in front of the entrance to the 'Holy of Holies' proved, when its plugs were removed, to have been filled up with a pair of fine goat's horns.

Plate 30

Similarly, there are many simple holes, conical perforations through paving or threshold slabs, that can hardly be functional in any way. Often they occur singly, but we may recall that at each end of the façade of the Tarxien temples there were the remains of a structure, the floor of which consisted of a slab containing several of these vertical perforations. Zammit, pointing out the presence of some stone balls nearby, inter- preted this arrangement as a ritual game in which the balls were lobbed into the holes. These balls, however, are of a type normally used by the ancient Maltese as rollers for moving their stone slabs (some of them can still be seen under the huge paving slabs in the outer right-hand chamber of the middle temple), and it seems to me more probable that the holes were intended for offerings, perhaps in this case libations or drink- offerings, to the dead, in the same way as some of the rope- holes. We may recall here the broken fragments of thousands of carinated bowls of phase E found in later temples, which surely served to contain some kind of liquid offering. Some of these simple conical holes, when they occur singly, have carved plugs, like the rope-holes. One of these holes, with plug, is found in the courtyard of the phase C temple at Mġarr though it could be a late addition. All these features, then,

Fig. 20

indicate a chthonic cult compatible with a cult of dead ancestors such as we have seen to exist in Malta.

The late temples have other and more specialized features, however: the altars and little cupboards or tabernacles of slabs, with or without central pillars. These also can be brought into relation with the ancestor cult, and are in fact merely a further elaboration of it, though perhaps their appearance in Malta is due to the influence of Aegean traders in the first instance. As early as 1901 Arthur Evans demonstrated that there was a close resemblance between the pillar niches of the Maltese temples, and the pillar shrines of the Creto-Mycenean civilization, and Albert Mayr remarked on the similarity of the mushroom-shaped monolithic altars at Haġar Qim to a common Aegean type of altar. We now know that these types of altar and niches first appear in the Maltese temples, quite suddenly, at the end of phase D or beginning of phase E, at a time when Aegean influence is beginning to permeate the whole culture of the islands. Nevertheless, they illustrate the point that a people only takes over from another what it can incorporate easily into its own culture. In Malta these congenial features are completely assimilated. In Aegean religion the pillar shrines are a symbol of the tomb and so of the dead ancestors; in Malta this symbolism is probably taken over, and they have sometimes been found, when undisturbed, to be filled with the charred bones of sacrificed animals, in this way symbolically offered to the dead. The altars themselves may be of various kinds, perhaps not all for the same purpose. Thus, the mushroom altars of Haġar Qim have a raised rim all around the top, as if to retain liquid. Of the altars which consist of a horizontal block, and which generally are set flanking the entrance to the passage from one set of rooms to the next, some at any rate served for animal sacrifices, as we saw in the case of the hollow one, more elaborate than most, from Tarxien, which was stuffed with animal bones. The sacrificial animals were cattle, sheep or goat and pig, as

Plates 8, 9, 10, 18, 25

Plate 16

shown by the bones themselves and by carvings of the animals. Of human sacrifices, it may be mentioned here, there is no shred of evidence to be found in Malta.

It is not possible to work out, from the over-all plan and arrangement of the Maltese temples, any very exact idea of the order of the worship carried out in them. On the whole, the floor-level tends to rise in the later temples slightly from the entrance to the back recess, generally in slight steps. Certain other things are also fairly constant, such as the position of the horizontal altars on either side of the passage, the greater elaborateness of the furniture of the outer set of chambers, the pillar niche in the back recess. But the plans of some temples, such as Ḣaġar Qim, are too aberrant for us to insist too much on this regularity of layout. The types of installation found in the chambers tend to duplicate each other, too, with almost monotonous regularity, so that we cannot recognize each as being appropriated to any one special purpose. The same rites, sacrifices and libations seem, so far as we can see, to have been performed in all. One or two features seem to hint at a division, in the later phases, between priests and laity. Some rooms at Tarxien, as we have seen, appear to have been shut off from the profane, and reached by a special approach intended for initiates. The so-called 'oracle' chambers at Mnajdra and Tarxien, with their separate entrances, cut off by all but a tiny window from the main chamber, must surely have been intended for some priestly purpose. But that is all the light we can obtain.

So far we have relied on the evidence supplied by the furniture of the chambers and the general layout of the temples as a whole. There is, however, a further very important source whence we can derive some idea of what the ancient Maltese religion was about, and what really went on in these mysterious, elaborate buildings like great tombs, yet in which no burials were made, namely, the objects found in the temples when they

Plate 18

Plate 26

Plate 21

were excavated. Among these, the most important for our present purposes are the numerous representations in stone and clay of human, superhuman and animal figures. Unfortunately, since they all come from old excavations, it is not possible to date them with absolute certainty in terms of the new pottery sequence. This, however, is not as serious a drawback as it sounds, because, with the possible exception of a tiny clay figure representing a cow found at Mġarr, it is highly probable that they all belong to the last two phases, if not all to phase E itself. The human and quasi-human figures are the most numerous and important, and it has been found possible to divide these into several classes and sub-classes. The main groups are (1) primitive figurines belonging essentially to types that are widespread in the Mediterranean, (2) stylized cult figures, (3) naturalistic human figures, and finally (4) small crude and deliberately distorted models. It will be convenient to deal with each of these classes in turn.

Into class 1 fall several types of small figurines which can be closely paralleled among the equipment of the early food-producing cultures in the Eastern Mediterranean. One type is represented by a tiny clay steatopygous figure from Tarxien, which can be exactly paralleled in the Neolithic deposits at Knossos in Crete and elsewhere. Another is a tiny bone object from the Hypogeum, which is identical in shape with the well-known 'fiddle-idol', a very much stylized human figure popular in the early cultures of Asia Minor and the Cyclades. Slightly less stylized types of Cycladic idol probably gave rise to figurines such as the two alabaster ones from the Hypogeum, though these are obviously of local manufacture and probably quite late. One of the types of cult figure which we shall be discussing later in dealing with class 2 was probably developed from idols of this type. Also belonging to this class are a small number of heads, more or less almond-shaped, with prominent triangular noses, and set on to the neck at the rather unrealistic

Plate 80, top centre

Plates 51, 52

Fig. 21

angle of about 45°; these once again recall certain characteristics of early Cycladic figurines. The significance of the foreign connections indicated by these figures will be discussed later in this chapter. For the present we will merely note that stylistically they are the most primitive of all the Maltese figurines, and also the only ones that show any really significant foreign influence.

Fig. 21   Two stylized clay heads, l. from Tarxien, r. from the Hypogeum. Actual size

Though the examples we have of them were probably mostly made rather late, their prototypes may well have come to Malta and been copied there much earlier.

The second class of figurines is one of the most important. These are purely Maltese in style, though they may have been developed from some of the types of class 1. Three varieties are known. The majority are naked, and represented either standing or squatting. These can be derived, respectively, from the flat fiddle idol and the squatting steatopygous figurine just

Plates 49, 50, 53

Plate 54

mentioned. A smaller number show a figure, clothed from the waist in a voluminous skirt, seated on a bench or chair. All these are stylized cult figures, almost certainly representing some kind of deity. Since they are made enormously and unrealistically fat, it is not difficult to recognize a symbol of fertility here, in the form it often takes among primitive peoples. A further characteristic which all these figures have in common is that they lack all sexual characteristics, male or female. That they developed from the more primitive types mentioned as class 1 seems on the whole likely, but where sexual characteristics are shown on these, either in Malta or abroad, they are normally feminine. Their complete absence on the more developed types of Maltese cult statuettes may imply that the being represented came to be regarded as asexual (somewhat like the Mediaeval angel). Figures of class 2, when well preserved, are invariably headless, but between the shoulders a socket is hollowed out to receive a separate head. Small holes bored through the walls of the socket indicate that the head was attached by means of a dowel, or by strings, which could no doubt be used to make

Plates 55, 56

the head move. Four heads suitable for statuettes of this class have been found, two in the Ġgantija and two more in the Hal Saflieni Hypogeum.

Plate 53

The best examples of the squatting figures are a series from Ħaġar Qim, though there are two others from Tarxien. They are all of stone, averaging about 8 in. in height, except for one much smaller example in clay, found at Ħaġar Qim. The hands rest symmetrically on the thighs, and the feet and calves are tucked up in some cases to the right, in others to the left. On one example from Tarxien, however, they are represented as coming down straight. In their massive calm these stone figures rather resemble figures of the seated Buddha, which may possibly be significant of the kind of impression they were intended to create. It has been suggested (by R. Levy) that the plan of temples of the later type was intended to reproduce

the form of these squatting figures. Though at first sight far-
fetched, there could be something in this idea.

The standing figures are less numerous than the squatting
ones, but much larger, and they vary more in size amongst
themselves. There is a good example from the Hypogeum, and   Plate 50
two from Haġar Qim, of which one is the largest and finest
specimen known. This figure stands on a pedestal, the front
of which is adorned with rows of drilled holes and painted red.   Plate 49
It was found only a few years ago, with some others, during
work conducted by the Museum at Haġar Qim. They were in
a position indicating that they must have been put aside and
forgotten by the early excavators. Their derivation from a
widespread primitive type is even clearer than in the case of
the squatting type. Their close resemblance to the two small
alabaster figures from Hal Saflieni has already been remarked   Plates 51, 52
on. These in turn are very like standing figurines of types well
known in Greece and the Aegean. The position of the arms
differs somewhat. Folded arms are typical of the eastern
Mediterranean figurines, whereas the Maltese statuettes have one
arm only folded across the breast and the other hanging
straight down the side.

The third type of cult figure differs materially from the two
types just discussed. Not only is it represented as clothed, but
also as seated on a sort of stool or couch instead of squatting on   Plate 54
the ground. Most typically the figure appears to be dressed in
a short, bell-shaped skirt which reaches half way down the leg,
and is seated on a too fragile-looking couch; this couch, when
the details are well preserved, seems to be identical with other
couches on which two female figures are shown reclining—as   Plate 57
in finds made in the subterranean chambers of the Hypogeum
to be discussed in full later when we come to the next class.
Around the sides, small figures are shown standing on the couch,
or cowering beneath it. Do they perhaps represent mortals
under the divinity's protection? We cannot do more than guess.

It looks very much as though the enormous fragment of a massive statue from the first court at Tarxien, mentioned above in describing the temple, probably belonged to this class. Although the surviving portion gives the impression of a standing figure, it seems impossible to avoid the conclusion that it was really seated, since it resembles the small seated ones in all details. Unfortunately, except in two cases, both of them rather anomalous, the body above the waist is broken off and missing in the statuettes of this class. Of the two in which the body survives, the one which approximates most closely to the normal type is dressed in what appears to be a gown with a U-shaped neckline. Around the neck there would seem to be some kind of heavy collar. For the rest, the gown is represented as quite plain, and (unusually) descends to cover the feet. Although the figure is evidently shown seated, no seat is indicated. The other figure is much odder. Though represented in front as naked, there is seen from behind what looks like the fringe of a decorated skirt. Part of a massive plaited pigtail can be seen descending the back. The head of the figure is missing.

Plate 54

Plate 63

The figures comprising this last group are difficult to ascribe, even remotely, to a more primitive prototype. They seem to have been rather the products of local religious developments, and have no direct forerunners either inside or outside the Maltese islands. All the figures described so far, belonging to classes 1 and 2, seem to be intended as representation of a divine being or beings, who probably personified fertility, and who certainly played a big part in the religion of the temples.

Class 3 covers more or less naturalistic representations of the human figure, and it is possible to discern within it two sub-divisions, namely, more or less clothed figures which one is tempted to call priests and priestesses, and naked female figures. There is no doubt that in each case we are dealing with ordinary human beings, indeed in a few instances they have the air of being real portrait-statues. The contrast with the stylized figures of the class just discussed is most marked. Sexual characters are strongly marked on the female figures.

Let us take the clothed figures first. To call these, as I have, priests and priestesses, may perhaps be regarded as unwarrantable, since, having no written records, we cannot prove that that is what they were. Yet this is the impression these figures have made on all students, and it seems inherently quite likely. The figures interpreted as priests are only three, and these are incomplete. They came from Tarxien, where they were found Plate 60 in a very delicate condition, being made of only very lightly baked clay; they had to be carefully reconstructed and consolidated. The figures are hollow inside and the surface very rough, as though it had been stuffed with straw. Their sex is inferential, since the chest region is missing in all cases, and the lower part of the body is covered with a bellshaped skirt, somewhat like that of the cult figures, but reaching to the feet. The dress alone, therefore, might lead one to imagine that they were a further variety of cult figure, were it not for the heads, which are preserved in two instances. The better preserved of these, when contrasted, for example, with the two stone heads from the Hypogeum, impresses one as being that of a male, and Plates 58, 59 very possibly a portrait. It may be mentioned also, in passing, that they were found in the inner part of the middle temple at Tarxien, the part supposedly cut off from the general public, which may be an argument in favour of their being priests.

The priestess figures are again few in number. They are represented, in fact, only by two examples, both found in the Hypogeum, apparently in one of the rooms with painted ceilings. They are very remarkable and puzzling figures, for Plate 57 each is shown reclining, the larger on her right side, the smaller on her face, on a couch identical in shape and construction with that on which the clothed cult figures sit. They appear to have a frame of wood, covered with reeds or canes. Each figure has a solid, woodenlooking pillow beneath her head. In this case at least there can be no dispute about the sex of the figures represented. The exuberant breasts of the larger and finer of the figurines leave no doubt whatever on that score. The smaller figure has lost her head, but the larger is complete, and is one of the finest pieces of modelling which the ancient Maltese have left us. She has been nicknamed the 'Sleeping Lady', and since the two figures do not differ in any very significant way, apart from their attitude, a description of her will stand for both. Though in the main treated naturalistically, the figure shows an exaggerated disproportion between the small head and upper part of the body, and the enormous swelling hips and thighs, which dwindle once more into relatively small calves and feet. She is naked to the waist, but the lower part of the body is covered by a three-quarter length skirt, which appears to be tightly constricted around the waist, and which is decorated with a curvilinear pattern and has a deep fringe at the bottom. The shape of this garment may be compared with the flounced skirts which women often wear in Cretan paintings, and the treatment of the whole body in this statuette, it has been suggested, might be regarded as an exaggerated rendering of the tightly laced figures in Cretan paintings and statuettes.

There are numerous examples of naked female figurines, more or less naturalistically rendered. They are less interesting and informative on the whole than the classes previously discussed, but they do include one masterpiece of modelling, namely the clay torso known as the 'Venus of Malta'. This figure represents a rather heavily built woman, with pendulous breasts and abdomen. The feet and head are unfortunately missing. The figure is at present 5 in. high, and the surface is highly polished and of a reddish-brown colour. She is represented in a standing position, with the left arm folded across the body below the breast and the right one hanging loosely by the side. The arrangement of the arms is reminiscent

Plate 65

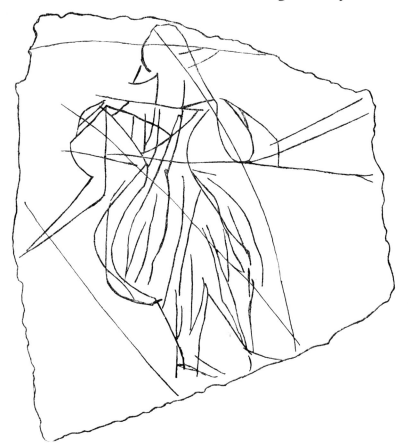

Fig. 22   Sketch of a corpulent 'dancing girl' scratched on a potsherd from the Tarxien temples. Height of figure 1¾ in.

of the standing cult figures of class 2, but in all other respects no greater contrast could well be imagined, for the 'Venus' is distinguished above all by the anatomical accuracy and meticulous realistic detail of the treatment. Part of the torso of a smaller clay figure was found in the Hypogeum. It makes, at first glance, a somewhat similar impression, but is in fact less detailed and more formalized in treatment. The upper part of the body must have excessively flattened, and the lower part of one of the legs, which was found separately, is distinctly clumsy. The initial impression, which is of something remark, ably like a Hellenistic figure, is therefore somewhat deceptive.

Two very small but rather remarkable pieces of modelling come from Tarxien. One is a strikingly naturalistic figure of a squatting woman made out of a tiny twist of rough clay. It gives the impression of having been an artist's 'jeu d'esprit' (compare the sketch of the fat 'dancing girl' mentioned in Ch. II, p. 76). The second is an even tinier piece representing two figures embracing each other. This is very roughly done (though it has been polished), but the subject is quite recognizable.

What really astonishes in these naturalistic figures we have been discussing, is the artist's eye for anatomy and pose. There is nothing comparable to be found in the archaeological remains from Western Europe for many centuries to come, whilst in the contemporary world one has to go to Knossos or Mycenae to find their equals.

Class 4 comprises crude and distorted figures and portions of figures, which we can only guess to have been *ex votos*, or else connected with magical activities practised for the hurt or healing of individuals. Prominent among these are the small clay figures representing horribly distorted female forms. One of these, reddish in colour, shows a female with pendulous breasts which hang down on to an enormously swollen abdomen. The backbone and ribs are shown as protruding, and the iliac regions as hollow and fallen in. The figure, found in the Hypogeum, apparently portrays the symptoms of a case of abdominal tumour. Another figure, very similar to the last, from Tarxien, has the further peculiarity that several sharp fragments of shell have been stuck into the clay at several points while it was still wet. What this may have signified we cannot,

Plate 61

Fig. 22

Plate 64

Plate 62

Fig. 23   The three leading figures (representing, right to left, a ram, a pig and a goat) of a procession of sacrificial animals carved in relief on a block of limestone in the Tarxien temples. Height of animals approx. 5 in.

of course, say with any assurance, but it certainly suggests some of the well-known procedures of sympathetic magic. Part of a similar roughly-shaped female torso, from Mnajdra, does not show the ribs and backbone in the same way as the former two, and may represent a different condition. A somewhat damaged clay head, from Mnajdra, with abnormally puffed-out cheeks also possibly belongs to this class, as may a small stone model of a hand from Ħaġar Qim, though the latter might simply have been intended as a kind of scoop. It is possible, too, that some rough twists of clay, vaguely resembling a pair of intertwined legs, which were found at Mnajdra, fall into the same category. All these figures would seem to be connected with healing cults, and possibly the practice of sympathetic magic.

Besides representations of human beings, models and carvings in relief of animals, birds and fish have been found in the temples. There is a small clay model representing a cow from Mġarr, already mentioned. In sharp contrast to this, which seems to be of a normal European type, are the humped cattle represented on the reliefs at Tarxien, and also on a sherd of a phase E bowl from the same site. A natural stone, possibly collected for its resemblance to a bull's head, was found on the

Fig 24   Stylized figurin *representing a bovid from t* *Hal Saflieni Hypogeum.* *Length 1 in.*

Fig. 25

149

Fig. 25 Figures of animals (humped cattle and a sow suckling her farrow) carved in relief on a slab of limestone in the Tarxien temples. Length of sow 7 ft 2 in., others to scale

surface near the minor temple of Hal Ġinwi a few years ago. Cattle which are probably of the humped type figure as part of the incised decoration of a plate from Hal Saflieni, and from the same site come some small models of cattle in shell and stone, which are, however, extremely stylized. Some of the latter may really represent sheep, as perhaps do the two primitive heads from Għar Dalam, and in one or two cases rams' heads are depicted on the ends of the high triangular plates which carry the handles on phase E strainer bowls. Two friezes in relief on slabs found in the left-hand apse of the first temple at Tarxien, figure respectively twenty-two sheep or goats, and four sheep or goats, a ram, and a pig. Sheep or goats also appear alongside the humped cattle on the plate from the Hypogeum mentioned above. Pigs modelled in relief appear on two sherds from Tarxien, which have already been mentioned in Ch. II (p. 80), and a sow with piglets is carved in relief alongside the two humped cattle at the same site.

Plate 75
Fig. 24

Plate 72

Fig. 11f

Fig. 23

Plate 75

Fig. 25

Apart from these domestic animals, which, as we have seen were also the sacrificial animals used in the temples, various others appear sporadically. Even shells were modelled in clay at Tarxien and Mnajdra. There are several representations of snakes, two on potsherds from Tarxien, one sculptured in relief on the front of a slab in the Ġgantija, and finally a snake's head made of stalactite, from Tarxien. A curious little figure of rough clay, called by Zammit a 'dog', seems really to be pretty evidently a lizard. A small piece of alabaster found at Tarxien shows two monkeys' heads set back to back. This, however, was found loose in the soil to the east of the main groups of buildings, and therefore could belong to a later period. Birds also are represented in various mediums. There are small stylized models of birds, whether 'doves' or 'ducks' is dubious, in shell and stone from the Hypogeum; a partridge-like bird is modelled in relief between a pair of horns on a sherd from Tarxien; and curious crested birds are

Plate 71

Fig. 26 *Stylized bird of shell from the Hal Saflieni Hypogeum. Length 1¼ in.*

Plate 73

151

Plate 74

represented in flight in several rows on a sherd of a phase E bowl found in 1954 under the platform at the Ġgantija. Finally, there are fish, which are represented in relief on the sides of a slab found in the Buġibba temple, and by two small models from the Hypogeum. One of the latter is of clay, and lacks head and tail, but is recognizable from the representation of scales and fins. The other is very curious. It is of soft stone, and shows a fish, modelled in outline, lying upon a couch of the type used by the cult statuettes and the 'Sleeping Lady'. I can think of no adequate explanation for this strange phenomenon.

Some of the creatures mentioned above may have had a symbolic significance. Snakes are known to have been associated with chthonic and fertility deities in many cults; the fish might well be a symbol of fertility. At the Buġibba temple, so close to the sea, it is quite possible that fish were the chief offerings made on the altars. The birds, too, and perhaps even the little lizard, had their significance, which, however, we cannot discern with any clarity at this distance of time.

Our survey of the human and animal figures found in the Maltese temples and tombs makes one thing abundantly clear —the complexity of the activities carried on in these in the later phases. We had already noted that, in addition to the propitiation of ancestral spirits and the cult of a fertility deity, some kind of wonder-working oracle was a feature of the phase E temples, and we can now add evidence of other minor

Plate 64

functions. The distorted and pathological figurines of class 4 can be reasonably interpreted as evidences of a healing cult. They were deposited in the temples either to solicit cure or as *ex votos* and mementos of a cure actually having been performed.

Plate 62

The sharp pieces of shell stuck into one of these statuettes are puzzling. They are reminiscent of the pins which in certain parts of Europe were, until quite recently, stuck into wax figures to injure or kill the person represented. This seems inconsistent with a healing cult such as I have just postulated, but, on the other hand, it is always possible that they were jabbed into the wet clay with the purpose of killing the disease and not the person.

The possibility of another practice, this time one which must have taken place in the gloomy inner halls of the Hypogeum, is darkly hinted at by the 'Sleeping Lady' statuette and its companion. These very curious figures may be explicable if they are regarded as models representing some activity carried out in the Hypogeum, rather than as objects buried as grave, goods with the dead. What this was we may conjecture, though we cannot know. In classical times it was the practice at some shrines for priestesses to give oracles and prophesy on the basis of dreams which they had whilst sleeping in some forbidding and mysterious place, for instance a cave. This practice is called 'incubation'. It seems possible, at least, that these strange figurines represent some such activity carried on by priestesses in the remote depths of the Hypogeum. Perhaps such visions were supposed to be inspired and sent by the dead, so that the Hypogeum would be the ideal place for it.

Plate 57

The Hypogeum is of course first and foremost a tomb, or rather a vast collection of tomb,chambers. By counting the number of individuals represented by the bones found in a small area, Zammit was able to calculate that about 7,000 individuals had been buried in it. Their remains were laid in specially deposited earth which filled both the chambers and the halls; this accounts for the presence of stone partitions between chambers or compartments, and also for the apparently sheer drops (most notably where the old part of the staircase to the third storey ends), since these were in fact non,existent when the original earth was in place.

The partition between chamber and chamber, and the curious oval enclosures (resembling 'opera boxes') to be found within some chambers prompts speculation as to whether there were special places of burial for sections of the community, perhaps clans or sub-clans. Be that as it may, the elaborate inner halls were evidently constructed with some additional end in view than the mere disposal of the dead, however ceremonial. The imitations of megalithic architecture, internal façades and elaborate painted ceilings all proclaim that. So in particular does the 'Holy of Holies' with its curious internal arrangements. It was mentioned in describing the Hypogeum that this chamber was evidently undergoing some sort of reconstruction and enlargement at the time when the Hypogeum finally became disused. Nevertheless, although the work was unfinished, a sort of temporary makeshift arrangement seems to have been made whereby the normal rites could be carried on. Thus, in what appears to have been a kind of underground pillar niche we can see a shallow circular depression to receive the base of a pillar, whilst above near the ceiling a kind of stone loop has been left, to which the top of the pillar could have been secured by a thong. This improvised niche evidently replaced an earlier one which was flanked by pilasters, and of which traces yet remain. Burials were certainly made in this chamber, but it was more than a burial chamber. This is emphasized by many details, such as the pillar niche inside, the holes in the door-jambs for the purpose of securing a cover across the door, the elaborately carved façade in front, and so on. Its ritual importance is further emphasized by the fact that no more chambers were cut beyond it, so that it stands at the limit of expansion of the structure. When extension was necessary, it had to take place downward, by the construction of the third storey. It is noticeable that the third storey does not pass the limit set by the 'Holy of Holies', but on reaching it returns on itself, spreading under the upper halls. Some holes set in line between the staircase to the lower storey and the 'Holy of Holies' seem intended to hold the framework of some kind of screen, suggesting that the mysteries of the latter were intended to be veiled even from those who entered the lower regions of the labyrinth.

Something of ritual observance, an extension of the rites performed in the megalithic temples, certainly penetrated into the Hypogeum in the fifth phase, though it seems unlikely that anything in the nature of general or public worship went on there, since there can have been very little light. Some light there obviously must have been, but the continuous use of a large number of torches would have left its marks in the blackening of ceilings and possibly of walls as well, of which there is no sign. It seems most likely, then, that the activity in question involved only a comparatively few privileged persons—priests and priestesses probably.

As was mentioned earlier, the much-battered remains of a megalithic building of sorts were found at the entrance to the Hypogeum. Though nothing could be made of the plan, it may be wondered whether this was not a temple or temple-complex in which the more public rites concerning the dead were performed. This speculation gives rise to the more general one as to whether all the great temple-complexes may not have risen above some rock-hewn resting-place of the dead, even if this might not always be as elaborate as the one at Hal Saflieni. Indeed, if the temple worship was, as seems to be the case, at bottom an ancestor cult, then one would expect to find temples in close proximity to the actual burial places. It is true that there is little evidence as yet to support this, yet there is some. The Hypogeum remains unique, but there exists a document written by an 18th-century Gozitan antiquary where a rock-cut labyrinth, which he claims to have explored under the Ġgantija, is described. Attempts to find the entrance to this have so far been unsuccessful, but there is no reason to doubt his word. A further piece of evidence might be seen in the rock-cut chamber at Tarxien which is entered by a shaft that opens under the destroyed right-hand portion of the small eastern temple there.

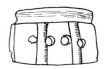

Fig. 27   Stone amulet from the Tarxien temples. It appears to represent a simple megalithic building. Length 1 in.

This might be a miniature example of the relationship between rock-cut and megalithic monuments.

Once we leave the sphere of religion and burial-customs we are faced with still more conundrums. Since all our finds come from temples or tombs, apart from a few from caves which may have been used for habitation rather than burial, our knowledge of all other aspects of ancient Maltese life depends on what inferences may be drawn from these. Our evidence is therefore very imperfect, and conclusions based on the material from temples and tombs about the daily life of the people could be misleading. To take one instance only, no trace of metal has been found on any of the sites. Does this mean that the Maltese temple-builders even of the later phases, when their neighbours had already entered the Bronze Age, really knew nothing of metal, or were metal objects perhaps merely excluded from entering the temples and tombs by a religious taboo? We know of similar taboos existing elsewhere. In this case the answer is probably that they really were without metal, except perhaps in the form of a chance import, such as the stone bead with pattern inlaid with gold from Tarxien. Nevertheless, this example illustrates the complexity of the problem.

Why no settlement sites have been found is a continuing mystery, since settlements of the later prehistoric period are relatively numerous. There are various possibilities. The modern villages perhaps stand on the same sites and cover them, or else the soil of the more fertile valleys may do so. Some remains may be hidden at the base of that great accumulation of debris on which rises the old capital of Malta, Mdina. Alternatively, the settlements may have been poor agglomerations of flimsy huts, or even tents, whose traces have long since vanished, their disappearance accelerated by the clearings and scourings of generations of Maltese peasants, covetous of new land to cultivate. Were all the inhabitants' superfluous energies, during the first period of Malta's history, concentrated on temple and tomb-building, to the detriment of house-building? But again, what is the meaning of a broken slab of stone which was found with the model façades at Tarxien? It appears to represent, in relief, the plan of a building composed of rectangular rooms, resting on a pediment composed of ashlar blocks. Not a temple, certainly, but perhaps a secular building, a palace? We cannot say; it tells us nothing that we can interpret with any confidence. For the only habitations of these people who built the immense megalithic temples and hewed out the labyrin-thine Hypogeum that have come to light are a few wretched caves which have yielded a little broken pottery and some animal bones. A strange paradox, certainly.

The economy of the early Maltese society was based, we can be fairly sure, on farming. The temples and tombs furnish abundant evidence of stock-breeding, in the form of bones and representations of domestic animals. Cattle, sheep or goat, pig, are all, as we have seen, well attested. Curiously enough, there seems to be no evidence for the oldest domestic animal, the dog. Agriculture is not directly attested, but may fairly be presumed. That the diet was supplemented by fishing may also be assumed in view of the representation of fish at Buġibba and in the Hypogeum, and also perhaps by a little hunting and fowling. Representations of birds are, as we have seen, found in the temples, and sometimes bird-bones are found there. Hunting is attested by finds of boars' tusks and deer antlers (a particularly fine antler was found quite recently when one of the carved altars from Tarxien was removed to the Museum). These could be imports, but it seems unlikely.

At the same time, lack of any weapons for hunting is puzzling. There are no spearheads, and only one rather inefficient-looking tanged chert arrow-head from Tarxien. A few other arrow-heads found in the temple-complexes almost certainly belong to the invaders of Period II, being of obsidian and of the hollow-based type. The only objects capable of being interpreted as weapons for the chase are the so-called slingstones, lentoid pills of limestone found in some numbers at the Hypogeum. Some of them may really be slingstones though they are rough-surfaced, whereas smooth stones are usually sought; others are too big and heavy, and are pierced at one end. The latter could perhaps have been used as weights for bolas. However, it is all very speculative and unsatisfactory. Lack of weapons for the chase implies lack of weapons of war, and certainly insofar as we can judge from the evidence, no more peaceable society seems ever to have existed. It is easy, of course, to delude oneself with pictures of a primitive Mediter-ranean paradise; nevertheless, the earth seems to have yielded the primitive Maltese a living on fairly easy terms, for otherwise they would scarcely have had time or energy to spare to elaborate their strange cults and build and adorn their temples.

And yet, although they strike us, judging from the remains they have left, as a kind of lotos-eating community, turned in on itself and wrapped up in its bizarre cults, technologically backward and cut off—in its tiny islands in the midst of the wine-dark sea—from the main cultural stream which flowed all about it, this is still only one side of the picture. It is easy to exaggerate the degree of their isolation. Zammit, going to the other extreme, imagined Malta as a kind of international 'sacred island' to which 'shipwrecked mariners' came to offer thanks for their survival. This was mere fantasy, for the temple cult was, as we have seen, a home-grown, earthy affair and the temples have yielded no collection of international nautical *ex votos*. Nevertheless, they have produced, as we have also seen, a fair amount of direct and indirect evidence of contact between the temple-builders and men of other lands, contacts which were made and kept up for purposes of trade in all probability.

That the Maltese must from the time of their original settlement have been engaged in active trade with other

countries is obvious and easily provable. The geology of the
Maltese islands is simple, and they lack many of the resources
necessary to a people even in a Neolithic stage of development,
such as flint, hard igneous rocks for axes, and red ochre for
colouring⁄matter. Among these, flint ranks as perhaps the most
basic. Coarse chert is indeed to be found in the limestone
formations, but we find real flint in use from the earliest periods;
this must have been brought from at least as far away as Sicily.
Sicilian contacts are clearly attested in the pottery of phases B
and C. By phase C at latest, the black volcanic glass, obsidian
is being imported, as shown by the piece found at Mġarr, and
this is most likely to have come from the Lipari islands, then
already a great centre for the export of this much desired
material. Confirmation of such contact with Lipari may be
seen in the half⁄dozen trumpet⁄lugs from pottery of the red⁄
Diana type which have been found in various temples, though
they might also have reached Malta from the north⁄east of
Sicily or even southern Italy.

During the period in which pottery of San Cono type was
in use in Sicily, contemporary with phase C in Malta, new
colonists with exotic cultural traditions arrived in Sicily, some
of them apparently related to the contemporary cultures of
Crete, the Cyclades and even Cyprus, and these ultimately
extinguished the old Stentinello/San Cono tradition there. Is it
perhaps from their influence that the head from tomb 5 at
Zebbuġ derived its Cypriot features? At all events, the new
Sicilian cultures had no influence on Maltese pottery, and to
judge by this, Sicilian contacts fall off completely in phase D,
though a few traits probably borrowed from the pottery of the
new traditions in Sicily can be discerned in Maltese phase E
pottery (in which phase also we find the carved oculus spirals
in Malta like those on Castelluccio tombs in Sicily). The
contacts which the phase D pottery, especially some of the
Xemxija material, does indicate are rather with south⁄east

Plate 48

159

Fig. 28

Italy, Sardinia and southern France, and there is good evidence that they continue into phase E. Many of the new types of pottery—studded wares, coarse unpolished wares with plastic decoration, etc.—could have been adopted in Malta under the influence of either south-east Italy or southern France, but the bowls with channelled decoration could only have been copied from the latter region.

Plate 43

Fig. 29

Further confirmation of trade connections in this north-westerly direction is not far to seek. The tunnel-handle may, as we have seen, have been adopted in Sardinia and France from Malta, but there are more certain proofs from the Maltese islands themselves. From Tarxien comes a fragment of a pot with a plastic cordon which is pierced along its whole length with holes at regular intervals. It is quite unlike any Maltese pottery, but identical with a type very characteristic of the culture of southern France and Liguria at this time. In the Hypogeum, moreover, there was found a small bead of greenstone in the shape of two spheres joined together, above which rises a small projection pierced with a hole for suspension. This is an unusual form of bead, known as a 'winged bead', and this example is unique in Malta, though the type is extremely common in the contemporary cultures of southern France and Liguria. To these undoubted imports we might add also the buttons of shell (and, in one instance, of greenstone) with V-perforation, of which one occurs as early as phase C in the Żebbuġ tombs, and the greenstone axe-pendants (miniature axes, perforated at the butt for suspension) which were found in large numbers at the Hypogeum and have turned up sporadically on other sites. Both these types are common to the west and north-west of Malta, in Spain, southern France and Sardinia, but not so common in Italy and Sicily.

Plate 83

Thus we can be fairly sure that the Maltese islands were connected by a web of trade relations that were more than sporadic with most of the neighbouring lands of the Western

Fig. 28 Sherd of reddish ware with channelled decoration from below the platform in front of the Ġgantija temples. Height 1¾ in.

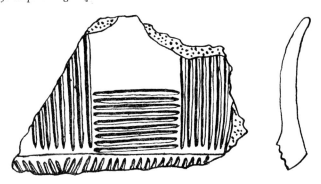

Mediterranean, some of which lay at a considerable distance. What the Maltese exported in exchange for the things they received from abroad it is somewhat difficult to determine. Certainly they had no natural resources to offer, and none of their pottery, carvings or statuettes has yet been found abroad. Their exports must therefore have been either intangible or perishable. Whilst not excluding the possibility that the ancient Maltese may have been known in their prehistoric world as great magicians, healers, men of spiritual power generally, it might also be suggested that textiles, or clothing of some sort may well have been among their exports. The islands were famed for their wool in Roman times, and though no spindle wheels attest the existence of a textile industry, we have excellent evidence of their skill in the manufacture of clothing in the statuettes, which also give us an insight into prehistoric Maltese fashions. Ancient Maltese costume seems to have begun generally at the waist, and to have consisted of a shaped and sewn skirt, sometimes quite elaborate, reaching either to the calf or to the feet; sometimes, however, as we saw in one of the seated statuettes, the upper part of the body may have been

Fig. 29 'Winged' or 'phallic' bead of green igneous rock from the Ħal Saflieni Hypogeum. Breadth ⅝ in.

Plates 57, 60

Plate 5

161

Plates 52, 55, 56, 58–60, 63, 70

clothed as well. Hair was worn straight and bobbed, or done in a way which resembles a barrister's wig, as in the case of the priest, or again in a long plaited pigtail, as shown on the headless seated statuette and on a head from Tarxien portraying a rather brutal and bull-necked individual. But was this actually the common dress, we must ask ourselves, or only that of temple officials?

Though the Maltese culture may have borrowed in some degree from various neighbouring cultures from time to time, it was not deeply affected by any of them, but went its own way. In its later phases, however, it came into contact with the Minoan and Mycenean civilization, through its traders who in the middle of the second millennium B.C. were setting up bases in the Central Mediterranean, notably at Lipari, and was profoundly affected thereby. No object demonstrably of Minoan or Mycenean manufacture has as yet been found on any of the Maltese sites, yet the culture of the final phase seems to have been saturated by the influence of Aegean civilization. The effect was nothing less than to transform it, though not to overwhelm it. It was the pinch of yeast which leavened the dough of the island culture.

Some of the main points which serve as indications of this Minoan/Mycenean influence have already been mentioned in the preceding chapters. Many others could be adduced and examples multiplied, but this would take up more space than it is possible to give to the subject here, important though it is. I must content myself with briefly indicating how all-pervading the evidence is. First, there is the change in building technique,

Plates 4, 5–11, 12–15, 20, 22

when rough, undressed lumps of stone yield to carefully cut slabs and blocks, with regular coursing and corbelling, which seems to come with the suddenness of a revolution. Then we noted the appearance, unheralded, in the late temples, of

Plates 7, 9, 19, 23–25

pillar shrines closely resembling those which played a great part in Minoan/Mycenean religion. The carvings in relief of spiral and spiral-derivative patterns which we find at Tarxien and other late temples have often been compared to the spiral-carvings of the gravestones of the shaft-graves at Mycenae. The idea of relief carving is certainly new in Malta, and may derive from this source, but the running spirals, apart from some at the Ġgantija, are closer to those painted on wall plaster and pottery in Crete in the Middle Minoan II and III periods than to the spirals at Mycenae. Others of the patterns in the Maltese carvings are merely based on the spiral, and seem to be local Maltese developments.

    The volute patterns constituting the basis of the decoration on the phase E scratched pottery and even some of its more complex elaborations can also be paralleled in Middle and Late Minoan pottery. In Crete the more elaborate of these patterns seem to be intended to imitate the veining of the stone which was also used for vessels there. One of the painted ceilings at Hal Saflieni, with its C-scrolls and loose running spirals has close parallels in the decoration of Cretan pottery and seals, as was clearly demonstrated by Sir Arthur Evans. Plant decoration, such as that found carved in relief on the 'floral altar' from Haġar Qim, can also be paralleled quite well in pottery decoration of the Middle Minoan period. We may note here also the similarities, already remarked upon, between the 'Sleeping Lady' statuette and paintings and statuettes represent-ing female figures from Crete. If this figure really represents a priestess 'incubating', we may well wonder if this practice did not reach Malta from Crete or Greece as well. The same might be thought about the healing cults. Both these were later a feature of classical Greek religion. The occurrence of bull's horns on the sherd from Tarxien, and the several representations of snakes on objects belonging to the last phase of the Maltese culture might again be due to Cretan influence, where both these animals are prominent as cult symbols. Finally, a very remarkable piece of evidence may be seen in several signs

Plate 25

Plate 44

Plate 31

Plate 79

Plate 57

Plate 73

163

engraved or scratched on objects datable to the last phase. A sign like the Greek letter Π with an extra foot occurs three times on different objects, once on a potsherd, once on an oval stone pendant (probably an amulet), and no less than four times round the surface of a fine cylindrical bead of dark greenstone. In the latter case it has been first incised and then encrusted with gold. This bead is very remarkable, since all the component materials, green stone, gold and the precious red stones, of which four were set in hollows around the surface and surrounded by rings of gold, must have been imported. A sign consisting of two triangles set apex to apex, perhaps intended as a double-axe sign, occurs once engraved on a sherd. Both these signs have approximate parallels in the Linear A script of Crete. Of course they are not writing in Maltese, but simply abstract signs, prob-ably with a magical or talismanic significance. But the fact that they were used and that they do resemble signs in Cretan writing does at least suggest that the Maltese had perhaps seen examples of this script.

Plate 85

It is noticeable that most of the best of the similarities mentioned above are with the material culture of Minoan Crete rather than that of the Greek mainland. Also they are with the later Middle Minoan, rather than the Late Minoan, period. Taken together these two facts may lead us to suppose that the people of Minoan Crete were already in contact with Malta somewhat before the rise of the Mycenean civilization in the 16th century B.C. This, if true, would probably mean that the transition from phase D to phase E in Malta took place some time in the 17th century B.C., which would fit the facts quite well. A few sherds of the early imported Aegean pottery found in the Lipari islands, datable to the 16th century B.C., are now thought to be possibly Cretan rather than Mainland, so this would give some support to the idea of a Cretan as well as Mycenean penetration of the Central Mediterranean. The idea of relief-carving, as we saw, may have reached Malta from the Myceneans rather than the Cretans, and may have come in late in the phase. There is none in the earliest phase E temple at Tarxien, and in the south temple at Mnajdra, which belongs to the early part of phase E also, the older type of decoration by drilled dots seems to have been the only one in use. Some of the simple geometric decorations used on Maltese pottery of advanced phase E type, such as concentric arcs and semi-circles, may also derive from the Mainland rather than the Cretan decorative repertory. Certainly the fifth and last phase of the Maltese culture seems to linger on into the 15th century B.C., that is well into the period of the supremacy of Mycenean trade in the Western Mediterranean.

The most important effect the contact with Aegean civiliza-tion had on the ancient Maltese is not, however, to be found in the borrowings of artistic motifs or religious paraphernalia, still less in the technological or economic sphere. It lies rather in the fact that in some strange way it awoke a latent aesthetic sense in them, with the result that we find a remarkably mature art developing among this people who in other respects, technologically for instance, and perhaps also socially, must be regarded as backward for their time and locality. All the productions of the Maltese culture of phase E bear the stamp of a definite canon of taste to which they conform, and this canon is not that of the Aegean civilization or any other, but one peculiar to the Maltese themselves. We can still recognize it and enjoy its qualities today in those masterpieces of Maltese work-manship that have survived to our time. Though it may be the size of the great temples which first strike us, it is the artistic achievement of the ancient Maltese which is ultimately most impressive, and which is their greatest claim to occupy a small corner in the memory of posterity.

The most remarkable feature of the Maltese aesthetic is its evident dislike of straight lines and sharp angles, its translation of all form into soft, sweeping curves. This is applied even to

Plates 15, 20–22, 29, 30

the slabs and blocks used in the construction of the temples, whose contours as far as possible are given a certain convexity. The same taste can be seen in the sweeping curves of the phase E pottery decoration, which is so graceful and balanced in the best pieces that it irresistibly reminds us of the exquisite Chinese Plates 39, 43, 44 pottery of the T'ang and Sung periods. In the Maltese pottery this preference for curvilinear decoration can be traced right Fig 4a back to phase B, when its unaccountable break-away from the rectilinear patterns favoured in Sicily can only be explained as a question of taste. Already in phase D this had evolved into a pleasing and vigorous style, though one which looks bizarre Fig 10 and barbarous enough beside the refinement of the phase E Plates 23–25, 28 productions. The abstract relief-carvings share the same qualities as the pottery decoration, and many of the patterns are identical, so little more need be said of them. Finally, there are the statuettes, in which the same canons of taste can be seen operating. They are best exemplified, perhaps, in the squatting Plates 57, 65 cult-figures, the Venus from Ħaġar Qim, and the 'Sleeping Lady'. The intricate balance of curved masses in these is reminiscent of the work of some modern sculptors, like Henry Moore and Barbara Hepworth. I have already stressed how effectively the former contrive to suggest a massive calm, a stillness which marks a vigorous creative energy. This balanced and finished art of prehistoric Malta is worth the consideration of anyone interested in the history of the aesthetic sense in man.

This, then, was the ultimate achievement of the descendants of those primitive farmers who crossed to the Maltese islands from Sicily several hundred years earlier, seeking no doubt a quiet corner of earth on which to live and produce their daily bread. In physical appearance the evidence suggests that they were a noticeably long-headed people, probably rather short in stature—typically 'Mediterranean' in fact. We know little of their economy, less still about their social organization. Their collective tombs and ancestor-cult suggest that they produced no powerful chiefs or kings, but lived rather in extended family or clan groupings. If there was any powerful class among them it was probably the priests who seem to have emerged by the last phase. The evident importance of women in their religion, as priestesses and possibly also in the person of the fertility deity (if she was in fact conceived as feminine) might tempt us into speculations about a possible matriarchal organization; but these had best be resisted, as they are likely to prove barren. Whatever their organization was, they perished obscurely, these people, some time just after the middle of the second millennium B.C. and became a mystery to future generations, as in many ways they are likely always to remain. We cannot claim that they contributed much, if anything, to the development of European civilization, but their art and their architecture remain for us as the permanent record of a single, small, but gifted community's interpretation of the raw material of experience; a particular pattern created out of the multitude of possible ones, which satisfied the spiritual needs of one human group for a time.

CHAPTER V

The Destroyers

THE REMARKABLE CIVILIZATION to which the preceding chapters have been devoted, after a long and unbroken development that can be traced through many centuries, finally disappears from view with great suddenness, and without leaving a trace in the material culture of Malta during the succeeding centuries. In its place we find the remains of what appears to have been in all respects a cruder and less advanced culture, except for its possession of some simple metal tools and weapons. The temple-builders vanish as if by magic, and we know them no more. The archaeological record, so often ambiguous as to the fate of individual cultures, is for once clear and unmistakable. Here is no gradual decline, no evolution of a culture into something different, not even the blend of a newly arrived dominant culture with survivals from the old. The temple-culture is seemingly at the very apex of its development when it disappears, sinking in the stream of time like a stone and leaving no trace. Its successor has completely different traditions, technological, aesthetic, religious. Nothing in the later prehistoric material warrant the assumption that any of the original people survived. If they did, they left no trace of themselves in the material remains of the new period. This is an unusual state of affairs. Zammit sought to account for it by supposing the islands depopulated by a plague, and later resettled by new people. But he thought there was a long interval between the two events, and we now know that this was not the case. On the whole, the grimmer alternative that the peaceful temple-folk were ruthlessly exterminated by the copper daggers and axes and obsidian-tipped arrows of the fierce invaders from across the sea seems more likely, though even this is only speculation. We simply

do not know what happened to them and probably never shall.

The new arrivals were the possessors of a culture which, though by no means so refined as that of the temple-people, has, to judge by the remains they have left, a strongly marked personality, the result of very different cultural traditions. These remains are concentrated at one site, the cremation cemetery found by Zammit in the Tarxien temples, and hence we generally refer to this people as the Tarxien Cemetery culture. For many years their origin was a complete mystery, but today we find ourselves much nearer a solution.

The material equipment of these Tarxien Cemetry people presents a lively contrast to that of the temple-folk whose remains lay at a lower level on the floor of the temple. Most abundant was pottery, in the shape of cinerary urns, and many smaller pots which accompanied these and probably contained offerings of various kinds. The paste and finish of these pots, as well as their shapes and decoration, are quite different from those of the earlier people. The clay is much coarser, containing large grits, and is less well baked. The pots are hand-made, like those of the temple people, but less regular, and they are covered with a thick slip, or outer layer of finer clay, which has generally been highly burnished with some hard object, such as a pebble or spatula, of which clear traces can be seen. This contrasts with the method of burnishing in the previous period which was done so as to leave no visible trace. In colour the new pottery varies widely from blackish or dark brown, and through several shades of red to an ochreous yellow—the most common colour.

The shapes of the pots are no less new and strange. The most common is a bowl or cup with broad heavy rim, turned outwards, which gives the vessel a rather clumsy, badly proportioned appearance. These bowls have a horizontally-pierced lug-handle on the shoulder and usually one or more warts as well. A variation of this, in which the bowl is oval in

Fig. 1 (12)

Fig. 30
Plates 89, 90

Plate 88

Fig. 30k

169

shape, with the lug set in the middle of one of the long sides, and the rim drawn up into a pair of triangular 'ears' at each end, is called a 'helmet-vase', and this type is usually elaborately decorated. Other cups and bowls have high strap-handles rising above the rim and are sometimes concave or 'winged' at the top. Single-handled jugs are common also; in these the rim

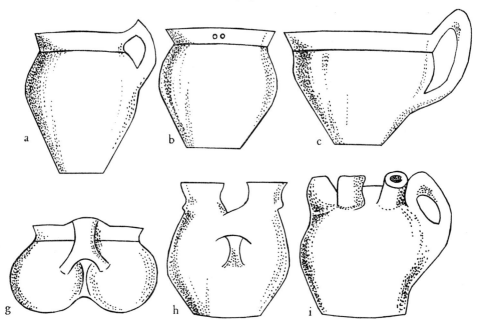

Fig. 30   Pottery shapes of phase IIA. Not to scale

is often higher at the point opposite the handle, and slopes down towards it. This is called a 'cutaway' neck. Frequently, on these, a kind of spout is made by drawing out two 'ears' at the point opposite the handle, producing a kind of 'hair-lip' effect. Jars with two and three handles are also found, as well as handle-less jars, the latter sometimes having two small holes close together near the rim, perhaps to fasten a cover. The larger jars constituted cinerary urns. Bowls of the type first described are sometimes mounted on a hollow conical foot; one is equipped with three small solid feet.

A part from these ordinary shapes, however, there are more bizarre types. Among these we may reckon askoi, or 'duck vases', double and triple vases, and double-necked vases. There

Fig. 30j, b

are also one or two examples of jugs fitted with a series of hollow tubular spouts arranged around the neck, and of curious basins consisting of a rectangular trough with a bowl at one end. The trough is divided down the middle lengthways either by a septum or by a bar supported at one end by the bowl and at the other by a pillar.

Fig. 30i

Fig. 33e

Most of this pottery is plain, or decorated only by a few knobs,

Plates 88, 90

warts, or applied disks; or alternatively by shallow dimples in pairs around the shoulder. Sometimes a pair of applied disks are surmounted by a V-shaped strip of clay producing the effect of a stylized human face, a sort of 'Chad' figure, which has many parallels in the pottery of other cultures. Vertical strips of clay set in groups are also used for decoration. About one-sixth of the pottery, however, bears an incised decoration. This is applied before firing, and generally consists of deeply scored lines, which are filled with white paste. But in some cases part of the decoration is made by applying the edge of a fossil shark's tooth of the kind that abounds in the limestone of Malta, or of the Noah's Ark shell. If impressed lightly, this produces a dotted line, and it was used for hatching to fill triangles and bands. The patterns are geometric and rectilinear, being made up of combinations of parallel lines and zig-zags, triangles, lozenges and metopes. From three to six parallel lines run horizontally around the shoulder of the vase, interrupting their course to form a large W-pattern at the base of the handle or lug. Below these generally come a number of parallel zig-zag lines which in the handle area may follow the upper lines or may cease entirely. The blank triangles between the upper parallel lines and the zig-zag ones are filled up in various ways, with smaller triangles or lozenges, or occasionally squares, and these are in their turn filled with fine hatching. Alternatively, the whole of the big triangle might be hatched, with the exception of a narrow inverted chevron outlined with incised lines and left blank. Sometimes a broad band was left between two sets of parallel horizontal lines, and this was filled up with a metope pattern in which alternate panels are filled with vertical lines and cross-hatching, or with parallel zig-zags. The pottery just described constitutes the bulk of the wares found in the Tarxien Cemetery, but there is also a small amount of fragments of a grey pottery, likewise decorated by incised patterns, which are sometimes filled with dots.

I have given this relatively detailed description of the pottery of the Tarxien Cemetery people to emphasize how very different it is from that of the earlier inhabitants of the Maltese islands, and to show that there is no question of a development of the one out of the other. The other aspects of the culture, insofar as we know them from the remains, reinforce this. A wide variety of objects was found along with the pottery and cremated bones in the cemetery at Tarxien. Of these a few are Period I objects re-used, but most are of quite new types. Notable among them are a series of copper objects, triangular daggers with two to four rivet holes in the butt for the attachment of a handle of wood or bone (a bone pommel for such a hilt was actually found), flat or slightly flanged axes with an expanded cutting edge, and awls of circular section with bone handles. Other metal objects were a thin sheet of silver with a biconical silver bead adhering to it, and a cylindrical lump of lead. An obsidian arrow-head of the hollow-based type shows that the bow was used. Other finds indicate that obsidian, flint and chert were used to make scrapers and blades, as in earlier periods. Spinning is attested by the presence of a number of spindle-whorls, mostly of clay, but occasionally of stone, and there is direct evidence of weaving in the form of some actual fragments of dyed cloth, made apparently of flax or some similar fibre. Some carbonized grain was also found. A sample of this recently analysed by Dr Helbaek of Copenhagen consisted entirely of horsebeans (*Vicia taba*), but Zammit reports that a sample which was analysed for him was said to contain barley as well.

Lumps of pumice-stone were also found which apparently served for sharpening the copper awls, to judge by the grooves in them. Though it is also frequently washed up on the shores of Malta, pumice may have been imported from Sicily; some sulphur which was found must certainly have been imported, and most likely from there. A lump of iron pyrites, which must,

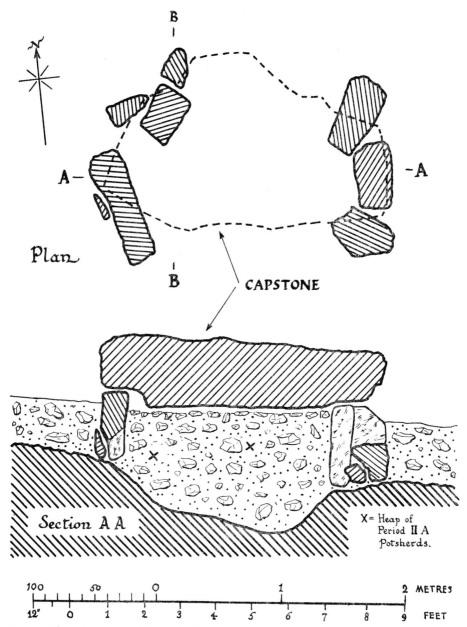

B

N

A —

Plan

B

CAPSTONE

Section A A

X = Heap of
Period II A
Potsherds.

100   50   0   1   2 METRES
12"   0   1   2   3   4   5   6   7   8   9 FEET

Fig. 31   Plan and sections of the 'dolmen' at Ta Hammut

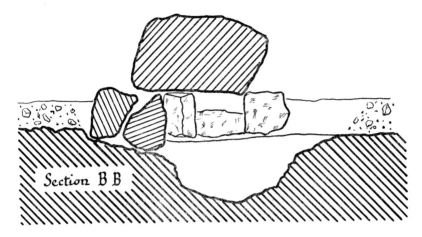

Section B B

like the flint, obsidian and sulphur, have been imported, was probably used as a strike-a-light. Other imports include the volcanic lava, used in the manufacture of quernstones.

Many beads, trinkets and amulets were found in the Tarxien Cemetery. Necklaces were apparently made of fish-vertebrae, and also of thousands of minute disk beads made either of ostrich-egg shell or faience, a blueish vitreous paste. Spacer-beads of stone, with a number of parallel perforations, show that the necklaces could be made up of several rows, each containing many hundreds of these minute beads. One fragment of a tubular bead of faience divided into several segments was also found; likewise, pendants of shell, hard stone and clay (the latter sometimes fashioned into the shape of birds or pots), which were probably interspersed with the beads in the necklaces. The finds included some large bone tubes, divided into segments by parallel grooves; they are of uncertain use, but were probably intended for adornment.

The religious life of the Tarxien Cemetery people has left traces in a series of curious clay idols, some of which are very stylized. Two, however, are recognizable as seated female

Plates 89, 91

175

figures, though even these are so far schematized that the arms and thorax have been fused together into a flat clay disk, and on the strength of these the remainder can be interpreted as further stylizations of the same subject. One of the two less formalized figures has an elaborate crescentic headdress, but the majority of the idols have not even a head. The body is represented by a flat disk with a dot at the centre, whilst the head and neck have been reduced to a thin triangular strip rising above it. The body is covered with an elaborate geometric incised decoration, and the legs, which have remained fairly recognizable, sometimes have their share of this as well. The less stylized pair of figures has certain affinities with some Mycenean types of idol, whereas the more numerous stylized figures are closer to Anatolian and Cycladic types, such as the fiddle-idol (of which we have already met with one example among the material from the preceding period).

Until recently the material just described comprised all that was known about the culture which succeeded that of the temple-builders in Malta and Gozo. A few fragments of similar pottery, and in one instance part of a stylized idol, were found among the debris on other temple sites, but no monu-ments built by this people were known. In the last few years it has been shown, however, that there are grounds for attributing to them a number of very small monuments built mostly of rough stone, whose age had hitherto been something of a mystery. Most of these are small chambers in which a single rough slab, often of considerable size, forms the roof; this rests on smaller stones sometimes made to form a wall around two or three sides of the chamber. For want of a better word these chambers were called 'dolmens', from their general resemblance to simple megalithic monuments in various parts of Western Europe, and they were vaguely associated with the temple-builders. Since most of them stand on bare rock and no archaeological material was found in them, it was impossible to go any further.

Plate 91

Plate 89

Plate 92

However, in 1955 I was able to investigate a very small monument of this type which still had some earth around it, and found some sherds of pottery of the Tarxien Cemetery style in the chamber. There was no pottery of any other type any⁄where near. This gives ground at any rate for a strong presump⁄tion that the 'dolmens' of Malta and Gozo were built by the people of the Tarxien Cemetery culture. Two years earlier I had also investigated a small rough stone structure of a different, but possibly related, type at Wied Moqbol, on the south coast of Malta. This odd monument, near which stand two others so dilapidated that one cannot make out whether they were originally the same or not, consists of a small oval chamber, which has a cairn of small stones, trapezoidal in plan, backing up against it on one long side, and two short lines of stones sprouting from the ends of the other. The chamber was found to contain pottery of Tarxien Cemetery type. It is therefore now possible to assign all the small rough stone monuments in the Maltese islands with a fair amount of probability to the people of the Tarxien Cemetery.

Fig. 31

There are about a score of known 'dolmens' in Malta and Gozo; these vary considerably in size, from the tiny one called Id⁄Dura tal Mara in Gozo, whose capstone is just 3 ft long, to that of Misrah Sinjura in Malta which has a massive cap⁄stone 12 ft square. The walls of the chamber for which the latter forms a covering are made of small dressed blocks of stone, but in this it is an exception. In most cases the capstone is supported simply by a few rough blocks. Most of the 'dol⁄mens' stand between 1 ft 6 in. and 3 ft high, but quite often the rock on which they stand has been hollowed out to a certain depth to increase the height of the chamber. We cannot be quite certain what purpose these 'dolmens' and cognate monuments served, since nothing that has so far been found in them gives us a direct clue. Nevertheless, it seems most likely that they were intended to be funerary monuments and once contained burials. The small size of most of them makes it probable that these must have been cremation burials, like those found at Tarxien. This would also make the disappearance of all trace of the actual burials more intelligible.

This is the sum of our knowledge about the Tarxien Cemetery people from such remains of them as have been found in Malta. It is not a very complete picture, but we can supplement it with a few details derived from a comparison of the remains with those of other areas. The first step in explaining them was the recognition of the close similarity between their pottery and that used by the Early Bronze Age people of the Lipari islands. This pottery (Capo Graziano ware, as it is called) is technically identical with that of the Maltese culture and some of the shapes are also very closely similar. In particular,

Fig. 30k, a, b there are the same broad-rimmed bowls, single-handled jugs with cutaway neck and small jars with pairs of holes just under the rim. At the same time, there are some notable differences in the material. The more elaborate and fantastic shapes among the Tarxien Cemetery range are lacking in Lipari, and the incised decoration of the Capo Graziano pottery is both simpler than that found on the Tarxien Cemetery wares (which more closely resemble that of the Moarda wares of north-east Sicily), and based upon a rather different selection of motifs, notably the dot and the wavy line.

The people who used the Capo Graziano pottery in Lipari were not indigenous there, however, but came to the islands from somewhere to the east. That they were already established there by about 1550 B.C. is shown by the Minoan and Mycenean pottery which is found stratified with their remains on the Acropolis of Lipari, but how much before this date they arrived is still a matter of guesswork. The similarities and differences between the remains of the Tarxien Cemetery culture in Malta and the Capo Graziano culture of Lipari strongly suggested that the relationship was a collateral one, and that each had reached its final home from some third area where the culture, which was the common ancestor of both, had flourished. The comparative dating of the cultures of the Maltese and Lipari sequences further implied that there must have been a gap of at least a century and a half between the Capo Graziano people's arrival in Lipari, and the coming of the Tarxien Cemetery culture to Malta. During that interval, the development of the ancestral culture in the hypothetical home land must have continued unbroken.

To locate this third area whence both the cultures came was a more difficult task. However, many lines of argument, based upon various pieces of evidence, combine to indicate that it was probably somewhere in southern Italy. There is, moreover, one very strong piece of evidence suggesting that the Tarxien Cemetery people at any rate set out for Malta from the extreme tip of Italy's heel. In this part of Italy, and only here, there are to be found 'dolmens' almost identical in construction with those of Malta. No material found in them has been published, but there are various details of the structures themselves which indicate their relationship to the Maltese ones. Besides general resemblance in appearance and range of size, it was found that numerous small details corresponded on the monuments of both groups. In each the capstones are frequently pierced with a vertical hole or scored with grooves on the upper surface, and the rock has sometimes been hollowed out beneath the Italian, as well as beneath the Maltese ones. This small and little known group of rough stone monuments appears to have no connections with the much larger and better known, though probably later, megalithic tombs that are scattered in the country between Taranto and Bari. They are centred on Otranto, and are not found further north than Lecce.

Although we know nothing of the people who built the Otranto dolmens, many resemblances can be traced between the pottery of the Tarxien Cemetery people and the Bronze

Age and Iron Age pottery of southern Italy which consider-ably reinforce the impression that they came to Malta from that region. In the last resort, however, the pottery of both the Tarxien Cemetery and Capo Graziano type can be seen to belong to a tradition of potting which has a long history, and can be traced back through Greece to Troy, Cilicia and Cyprus. Bossed bone objects, which probably have some ritual significance, and of which one appeared at Tarxien, and clay anchor-shaped hooks—both of which may have formed a part of the material culture of the Tarxien Cemetery people, though this is not quite certain,—would lead us back in the same direction, for they are both found in Greece and in the Troad. A full study of the complex origins of the Tarxien Cemetery culture, therefore, would take us too far afield. Nevertheless, the more we get to know about these people the more fascinating their history becomes, and the stranger appears the fate which ultimately led them to settle in the Maltese islands.

However they may have obtained possession of their new home, the Tarxien Cemetery people did not long continue to enjoy their prize in peace, for shortly they themselves were overwhelmed by an influx of people who appear to have made the crossing to Malta from Sicily. This new invasion probably took place not much more than a century after the arrival of their predecessors in the islands. We can be reasonably certain about this because of the contacts with Mycenean traders which are attested in the material remains of both cultures. The Tarxien Cemetery people wore necklaces containing blue faience beads of types that were being distributed in Europe by Mycenean trade in the 14th century B.C., whilst among the remains of the new invaders on the site which gives its name to the culture, Borġ in-Nadur, was a small fragment of Mycenean pottery, *Fig. 34* probably part of a stemmed goblet, or *kylix,* which can be assigned to the Mycenean IIIb phase, datable to the 13th century B.C.

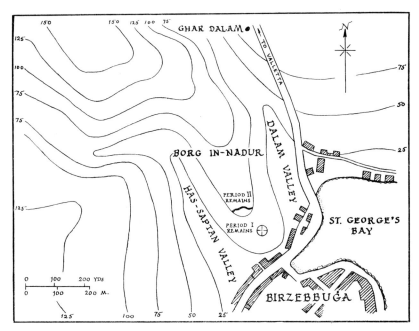

Fig. 32   Plan showing the relative positions of the Period I temple and the phase IIB defensive wall at Borg in-Nadur

The second invasion of the Maltese islands must therefore have taken place at some time during the 14th century B.C. This time it looks as though the new arrivals had to fight for possession. Their remains have been found at a number of sites on the Maltese islands, some of them settlements, which are always naturally defensible, and sometimes made more so by means of massive stone walls. A fairly large number of tombs are also known. These are bell-shaped chambers cut down into the rock and entered from above; sometimes they are within the area of a settlement, sometimes outside. Many have been cleared out, lined with plaster and re-used as cisterns, but some are undisturbed. Two of these, accidentally discovered in 1939 on the Mtarfa promontory near Rabat, were excavated by

Mr J. B. Ward Perkins and one yielded a large amount of characteristic pottery.

Some of the settlements of this period are on the flat-topped hills which occur here and there in Malta, and are much more common in Gozo. In-Nuffara, a hill situated opposite the hill of Xagħra on the slopes of which stands the Ġgantija, has a characteristic settlement of this kind. Others are in more or less triangular promontories, generally formed by the joining of two *wieds* or dry river beds, and this type usually has a defensive wall on the undefended side. Examples are Guardia ta San Gorg and Borġ in-Nadur. The last-named has by far the most massive remains of a defensive wall of any, and it has given its name to the culture as a whole. It is a triangular promontory of the usual type, close to the edge of a small creek called St George's Bay on the north-west side of the Marsaxlokk.

Fig. 1 (25)
Plate 93

A temple, previously mentioned, had already been erected on this promontory probably late in Period I. Excavations made in the ruins of this building by Dr Margaret Murray in the 'twenties showed that it was incorporated by the newcomers into their settlement. Within its once-sacred precincts the women ground flour and cooked, as shown by the numerous hand-mills, mortars and traces of fire found by the excavators. No definite traces of houses are known, but there is some evidence that Caruana probably found the remains of at least two oval huts in his excavations here just behind the massive defensive wall.

Fig. 32

Great quantities of pottery were found by Dr Murray in her excavation of the temple area, all but a very little of it of the type brought with them by the new settlers. It is of a kind completely novel and strange to the Maltese islands. Almost all of it is made of a buff-coloured paste (grey at the core, generally, due to poor firing), covered with a rather shiny red slip, which has a tendency to crackle and flake off in small pieces. The range of shapes made in this ware is large, and all

Fig. 33

hitherto completely unknown in Malta. Most frequent are basins with a flat base and two small ring handles, and a variation of this in which the whole is set on a high conical foot. There are also cups with high handles, bowls with a strap⁄handle, footed cups and lamps, single⁄handled jugs, and jars

Plates 94, 95;
Fig. 33

Fig. 33d, b, c, f, g, a

Fig. 33   Pottery shapes of phase IIB. Not to scale

of various sizes with four strap⁄handles. The largest of the latter are about 3 ft high. Finally, there are many fragments of rectangular basins, which are divided up internally in the same way as those already described in dealing with the Tarxien Cemetery culture. This is the only shape common to the two cultures, though the ware of course differs completely. A

Fig. 33e

Plate 95

Plate 94

curious feature are the Y/ or T/shaped handles, which are often found, but never on a complete vase; they were probably attached to little conical cups. Other unusual types of handle are those with an axe/shaped projection on top, and ordinary ring handles divided by a piece of clay across the centre into two halves. Decoration consists of deep grooves, square in section and filled with white paste, and occasional deep dots. The patterns made with these are simple. Applied pellets of clay are also sometimes used for decoration. The use of decoration of any kind is always sparing on these vases, and many are not decorated in any way.

Basins and footed bowls identical with those found at Borġ in/Nadur and elsewhere have been found in Bronze Age rock/tombs which form large cemeteries near Syracuse, in Sicily. In these they are associated with a grey pottery that is much more common, and with imported Mycenean pottery. Dr Bernabò Brea has concluded that these pots represent imports into Sicily from Malta, but whether this be so or not, I find myself unable to agree with the implication that the Borġ in/ Nadur culture is essentially Maltese. As I have pointed out above, the whole of the pottery is essentially alien to previous Maltese traditions, whereas it has numerous parallels in Sicily. Buff wares covered with a flaky red slip have a long history in that island, which goes back to the very beginning of the metal age there, shortly after 2000 B.C. Some of the shapes later found in the Borġ in/Nadur pottery can be traced back thus early in Sicily, notably that of the divided basins. It therefore seems to me likely that the tradition of these red wares continued unbroken in some of the lesser known parts of the island long after it had died out in the Syracuse region. Red wares make a spectacular come/back in the Sicilian material after about 1200 B.C., and it seems almost certain that their line of descent is unbroken. It must always be remembered that many parts of Sicily are still not well explored archaeologically, and we

may expect more light to be shed on this question by future work.

In view of these facts, I feel quite justified in holding that the Borġ in-Nadur people came to Malta from Sicily, probably from some part of the south coast of that island. It is tempting to see in the site of Borġ in-Nadur itself, which lies so close to the shore, their original beach-head in Malta, though of course this is merely speculation, and we can never know if this was so or not.

The great defensive wall that defends the landward side of the Borġ in-Nadur promontory is as unusual in plan and technique of construction as the rest of the equipment of the new people. The whole central portion of the wall describes a wide arc which is almost a semicircle, and only the two ends are more or less straight. It is rather like a huge bastion, and perhaps served a similar purpose by enabling the defenders to enfilade other parts of the wall. In the best-preserved parts the wall is about 12 to 14 ft high at present, and it averages 4 to 5 ft in width. The type of construction varies from one part to another. Mostly it consists of large rough blocks arranged in very rough courses, the spaces between them being packed with small stones dressed to fit. In some parts, however, a few large blocks only are used, being set as uprights or transversely to tie the inner and outer faces together, and the rest of the wall consists of smaller irregular dressed blocks.

Fig. 32

Plate 93

The Borġ in-Nadur wall finds its best parallel, like the pottery, in Sicily, where there is a somewhat similar defensive construction at Monte Finocchito, which may, however, have been built later than the Maltese example. It shows nevertheless that the tradition of this kind of construction, as well as that of red pottery, was well established in Sicily. It may also be noted, however, that there is a quite perceptible resemblance between the construction of some parts of the walls of Mycenae itself and that of Borġ in-Nadur.

185

People who carried on the tradition of the Borġ in-Nadur culture seem to have occupied the Maltese islands undisturbed for several centuries. During that time their red-slipped pottery

Fig. 34   Drawing of a Mycenean chalice, showing how the sherd of Mycenean pottery from Borġ in-Nadur would fit into a vessel of this type

underwent changes which we can link with developments outside Malta, in Sicily and the Italian mainland. So far as can be seen these changes were gradual and peaceful, and imply no interruption of life on the islands. The most obvious change is in the colour of the pottery, which changes slowly from red on buff to black on grey. The decoration changes too, becoming more profuse (although a large proportion of the pots are still plain), and beginning to acquire new motives, such as the spiral and meander, concentric circles, and zig-zags executed in a technique known as excision, or chip-carving. Originally a wood-carving technique, this consists of cutting out the

Plates 96, 97

186

background and leaving the pattern standing in relief. The site that has produced the greatest quantity of this black, chip-carved pottery is Bahrija, a settlement-site on a hillside near the south-west coast of Malta, after which the phase is named. The site was the scene of a short trial excavation by T. E. Peet in 1909, but has not been re-investigated since. It was naturally defensible, like the Borġ in-Nadur ones, but a few traces of *torba* floors were the only remains of constructions found.

Fig. 1 (26)

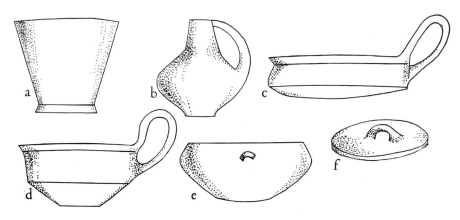

Fig. 35   *Pottery shapes of phase IIC. Not to scale*

Typical shapes of the Bahrija pottery are shallow bowls with inturned rim, carinated bowls with a high strap-handle, also jugs and jars and fragments of what Peet describes as rectangular boxes. There were, too, a few fragments of painted wares. Clay anchor-shaped objects which were found on this site, as also at Borġ in-Nadur, have parallels in the Middle Bronze Age culture of the Lipari islands, but they may really belong to the earlier Tarxien Cemetery culture, small amounts of whose characteristic pottery was found on both these sites.

Fig. 35e, c, d, b

Some of the shapes, for instance the high-handled bowls, connect the Bahrija culture with the Late Bronze Age Ausonian

Fig. 35c, d

187

Plates 96, 97

culture of Lipari. This culture probably reached Lipari from the Italian mainland, and other features of the Bahrija pottery, such as the use of meander patterns and chip-carving, connect it more directly with the Late Bronze and Early Iron Age cultures of the mainland. Some decorated clay weights have very close parallels from the Early Iron Age site of Canale Ianchina in Calabria. Further, a bridge-spout decorated with an animal's head is also an imitation of a mainland type. The few painted sherds, on the other hand, find their closest parallels in Late Bronze Age Sicily.

It seems fairly clear from the range of foreign parallels that the Bahrija phase in Malta must begin a little before 1000 B.C. and continues until the islands were colonized by Phoenicians from Carthage in the 8th or 7th centuries B.C. The Phoenicians, of course, are a people known to us, however imperfectly, from written sources as well as from archaeology, so that with their arrival this study of the prehistory of the Maltese islands may fitly end, even though no actual written records that date back to before the 3rd century B.C. have been found there.

No study of the prehistory of the Maltese islands would be complete were it not to devote a few paragraphs to the problem of the so-called 'ancient cart-tracks' which are such a well-known sight on the bare rocky hillsides and plateaux of Malta and Gozo. Because they are very difficult to date, and cannot be definitely proved to be the work of any one of the cultures dealt with above, I have thought it better to describe them in an Appendix.

These tracks may be seen at many points where the rock is exposed, and can often be followed over quite long distances. From the air they give the impression of a railway network, with junctions and marshalling-yards at intervals. Sometimes many pairs of tracks run parallel, at other times they cross each other at various angles, running in different directions. The tracks of each pair are about 55 in. apart on an average, though there is a variation of several inches each way.

Many fantastic legends have gathered about these curious tracks, such as that they run on under the sea to Sicily—or even North Africa! There are indeed places where the tracks end abruptly on a cliff edge, or run down into the shallow water of an inlet on the coast, but this is due simply to the normal geological processes of weathering and subsidence during the many centuries since the tracks were first formed, and really give no support to any more startling hypothesis.

Very little serious study of the tracks has been carried out. Papers on the subject were published by Captain E. G. Fenton, and later by Sir Themistocles Zammit, but the most recent, and, I think, most successful work on them has been done by Captain H. S. Gracie, R.N. The conclusions of the last-named are somewhat startling, but, I believe, convincing. The ancient tracks, he points out, are quite unlike modern cart-ruts. They are V-shaped in section, slightly rounded at the bottom, and often quite deep, whereas ruts made by modern carts (which can also be seen at many points where the rock is exposed) are broad, shallow and flat-bottomed. Captain Gracie marshals many arguments to show that the tracks could not have been made by a wheeled vehicle. Apart from questions of depth and section, he points out that the tracks often curve sharply in such a manner that wheels would have stuck, and suggests that the vehicle which left such tracks must have been a slide-car, a form of transport which was widely used in Europe and Asia until quite recently. This consists of two wooden shafts supported at the front ends by the draft animal (generally a horse or ox), while the rear ends trail along the ground. The shafts widen towards the 'heels', and somewhere in the middle is the body of the cart, often made of wickerwork.

In 1955 it was possible to test this theory practically during the preparation of a television film about Maltese prehistory. A pair of cart-wheels and a specially constructed slide-car were drawn along some well-preserved sections of tracks. The wheels jammed continually, whereas the slide-car ran easily, fitting the tracks admirably, and thus demonstrating that such a vehicle could have made them.

At present the surface of the exposed rock is so hard that such deep ruts would scarcely be made, but Captain Gracie points out that the Maltese limestone is quite soft when covered by even a thin layer of soil, though it develops a hard patina when exposed directly to the atmosphere. The tracks must therefore have been made when soil still covered the bare hillsides, which is incidentally a useful piece of evidence to support the idea that the islands were once less barren than they now are.

This leads on to the question of dating. Tracks are interrupted by graves of the Punic period cut in the rock at several places, and at one at least of these the lip of the rut is a sharp right-angle, indicating that the track is older than the grave. Though the grave itself is not more precisely datable, it seems to afford some evidence that the tracks had gone out of use in the Punic period and are therefore prehistoric in date.

Zammit claimed that they belonged to the Neolithic (our Period I), but there is no evidence to support this. They noticeably do not occur near some of the main temple-complexes, though these are surrounded by bare rock. On the other hand, they are often found on or near the promontories and hill-tops on which sites of the Borġ in-Nadur and Bahrija cultures occur, which might indicate that they were in use during Period II. Both Captain Fenton and Captain Gracie think that they must have been made during a period of wetter climate than the present.

The tracks evidently formed an elaborate communication-system, and to judge by their numbers, probably served a fairly large population. Zammit thought that they were used by vehicles for taking soil up the hillsides for use in making terraces, but in fact the tracks do not run simply from the valleys up to the hills. Some of them keep to the hills, others skirt them, keeping to the low ground. Probably they were used to transport many different kinds of goods from settlement to settlement.

Finally, it may be worth adding that ancient 'cart-tracks' have been reported from other countries besides Malta. Many are known in Sicily, though they have not been carefully studied, and this might be an argument in favour of connecting them with the Borġ in-Nadur people in Malta. They also apparently occur in southern France and Greece.

Appendix II: Seeing the Prehistoric Remains of Malta

In the main body of the book I have tried, with the aid of the photographs and drawings, to describe the material remains left by the prehistoric inhabitants of the Maltese islands, especially the earliest of these. But nothing is so rewarding as to see them for yourself. The Maltese temples are exciting to visit, and some of the things found in them are almost equally fascinating to see in the Museum.

The main collection of Maltese antiquities is in the National Museum, which is now housed in the Auberge de Provence (once one of the hostels of the Knights of St John), which stands in Kingsway, the main street of Valletta. From its displays you can obtain a very complete picture of the material found on the sites of the various prehistoric cultures of the islands. There are also two small subsidiary Museums at the site of the Tarxien temples and the Hal Saflieni Hypogeum respectively. A few objects, including two large and fine, but much-weathered heads of large statuettes, from the Ġgantija, are preserved in the Public Library at Victoria in Gozo. A new Museum is, however, in preparation within the walls of the old town.

Most of the main monuments are not difficult to get to, Tarxien and Hal Saflieni being among the easiest. They can both be reached by taking a bus from Valletta to Pawla, on the other side of the Grand Harbour, and getting off in the Square; from there it is quite a short walk. The Hypogeum is, appropriately enough, in Burials Street, and is entered through a 'neo-Megalithic' portal. The Tarxien temples are a little further away, and here again part of the protective wall around them is in the 'neo-Megalithic' style. The south building at Kordin can also be reached by means of the Pawla bus, and alighting just after it turns up the hill to Pawla, having passed the Marsa; but to visit this building, which has no custodian, the key must first be obtained from the authorities at the National Museum.

Ħaġar Qim and Mnajdra can conveniently be visited together. There is a relatively frequent bus service from Valletta to the village of Qrendi, and from there the temples can be reached in about fifteen minutes on foot. Recently a good highway for cars has been completed which leads up to the gates of Ħaġar Qim.

The most difficult of the temples in Malta to reach are those at Mġarr. Buses do run to this village from Valletta, but they are infrequent, so times should be ascertained in advance. For those with cars, of course, no difficulty arises. Any site in Malta may be reached in about half an hour. Once in the village, the rest is easy. The temples are approached down a narrow lane, which opens on the left off the main street, opposite the school.

To visit the Ġgantija with comfort you must be prepared to spend a night on Gozo—no great hardship, since it is a most attractive island. The ferry crosses from Marfa, at the north-west end of Malta, which can be reached by bus or car. The ferry will take private cars across, but it is advisable to book beforehand. There are hotels at Mġarr, the little port in Gozo where you land, or you can stay in Victoria, the chief (or rather the only) town. From either of these the Ġgantija on its hillside can be visited in the course of the day, and the return journey made the following morning—unless you wish to see more of the island, and enjoy the excellent bathing it offers.

The modern Maltese orthography followed in this book is completely phonetic; each letter or combination of letters has its special function, and each stands for one, and only one, sound. Most of the letters present little difficulty, but there are some which have been modified to represent special Maltese sounds, and a few others whose Maltese pronunciation is very different from their English one.

Several letters of the Maltese alphabet are written with a dot above which serves to soften them. Thus ċ is pronounced as ch in 'church' (the ordinary c is not used), and ġ as j in 'James' (the ordinary g being hard, as in 'golf'); ż is pronounced as in 'zone', whilst the ordinary z has a 'ts' sound, as in 'hits'.

The Maltese h is silent as in the English 'hour', except at the end of a word, when it is strongly aspirated. Elsewhere in a word the sign ħ, Ħ is used to indicate an aspirated h.

The combination għ represents the purely Semitic sounds of the Arabic 'għain' and 'rgħain'. No distinction is made between these in Maltese, and the letters do not have a distinct consonantal sound, but simply colour the following vowel.

J is pronounced like English y in 'young'.

Q represents the Arabic 'qâf'. In Maltese it is pronounced as a kind of glottal stop.

X is pronounced sh as in English 'shower'.

Bibliography

General Background

L. BERNABÒ BREA, *Sicily before the Greeks*, Ancient Peoples and Places Series, No. 3. London, 1957

G. E. DANIEL, *The Megalith Builders of Western Europe*, London, 1958

Geology

H. P. T. HYDE, *The Geology of the Maltese Islands*, Malta, 1955

Maltese Prehistoric Antiquities

G. F. ABELA, *Della Descrittione di Malta*, Malta, 1647

G. F. ABELA, *Malta Illustrata ovvero Descrizione di Malta* (enlarged edition with copious notes by G. A. Ciantar), 2 vols, Malta, 1772–80

J. HOUEL, *Voyage pittoresque des Iles de Sicile, de Malte, et de Lipari*, Vol. IV, Paris, 1787

L. MAZZARA, *Temple anté-Diluvien des Géants dans l'Ile de Gozo*, 1827

A. DE LA MARMORA, 'Lettre à M. Raoul Rochette sur le temple de l'Ile de Gozo, dit le Tour des Géants', *Nouvelles Annales publiées* par la section française de l'Institut Archéologique, I, 1836

J. G. VANCE, 'Ancient Temple near Crendi, Malta', *Archaeologia*, Vol. 29, pp. 227–40

A. L. ADAMS, *Notes of a Naturalist in the Nile Valley and Malta*, Ch. V, Edinburgh, 1870

J. FERGUSSON, *Rude Stone Monuments*, Ch. XI, London, 1872

J. H. COOKE, *The Har Dalam Cavern, Malta, and its Fossiliferous Contents*, Malta, 1893

A. MAYR, 'Die vorgeschichtlichen Denkmäler von Malta', *Abhandlungen der k. bayer. Akademie der Wissenschaft, I Cl., XXI Bd., III Abth.* (Shortened and revised version published in English under the title 'The Prehistoric Remains of Malta' in 1908)

A. MAYR, *Die Insel Malta im Altertum*, Munich, 1910

T. E. PEET, 'Contributions to the Study of the Prehistoric Period in Malta', *Papers of the British School at Rome*, Vol. V, No. 3, pp. 141–63

N. TAGLIAFERRO, 'The Prehistoric Pottery found in the Hypogeum at Hal-Saflieni, Casal Paula, Malta', *Annals of Archaeology and Anthropology, University of Liverpool*, Liverpool, 1910.

T. ZAMMIT, 'The Hal Saflieni Prehistoric Hypogeum at Casal Paula, Malta', First Report, Malta, 1910

N. TAGLIAFERRO, 'Prehistoric Burials in a Cave at Bur Meghez, near Mqabba', *Man*, 1911, pp. 147–50

T. ZAMMIT, T. E. PEET and R. N. BRADLEY, 'The Small Objects and the Human Skulls found in the Hal Saflieni Prehistoric Hypogeum', Second Report, Malta, 1912

T. ASHBY, R. N. BRADLEY, T. E. PEET and N. TAGLIAFERRO, 'Excava-tions 1908–11 in various megalithic buildings in Malta and Gozo', *Papers of the British School at Rome*, Vol. VI, 1913, pp. 1–126

G. DESPOTT, 'Excavations at Ghar Dalam (Dalam Cave), Malta', *Journal of the Royal Anthropological Institute of Gt. Britain and Ireland*, Vol. LIII, 1923, pp. 18–35

T. ZAMMIT and SINGER, 'Neolithic Representations of the Human Form from the Islands of Malta and Gozo', *Journal of the Royal Anthropological Institute of Gt. Britain and Ireland*, Vol. LIV, 1924, pp. 67–100

M. A. MURRAY (and others), *Excavations in Malta*, 3 Parts, London, 1923–9

T. ZAMMIT, 'The Ta Ħaġrat Megalithic ruins at Mġar, Malta', *Bulletin of the Museum*, Vol. I, 1929, pp. 5–25

T. ZAMMIT, *Prehistoric Malta, The Tarxien Temples*, Oxford, 1930

M. A. MURRAY, *Corpus of the Bronze Age Pottery of Malta*, London, 1934

L. M. UGOLINI, *Malta Origine della Civilta Mediterranea*, Rome, 1934

J. B. WARD PERKINS, 'Problems of Maltese Prehistory', *Antiquity*, Vol. XVI (1942), pp. 19ff

J. D. EVANS, 'The Prehistoric Culture-Sequence in the Maltese Archipelago', *Proceedings of the Prehistoric Society*, Vol. XIX, 1953, pp. 41–94

J. G. BALDACCHINO and J. D. EVANS, 'Prehistoric Tombs near Zebbug', *Papers of the British School at Rome*, Vol. XXII (N.S. IX), 1954, pp. 1–21

H. S. GRACIE, 'The Ancient Cart-tracks of Malta', *Antiquity*, Vol. XXVIII, 1954, pp. 91–8

J. D. EVANS, 'The "Dolmens" of Malta and the Origins of the Tarxien Ceme, tery Culture', *Proceedings of the Prehistoric Society*, Vol. XXII, 1956, pp. 85–101

D. WOOLNER, 'Graffiti of Ships at Tarxien, Malta', *Antiquity*, 1957, pp. 60–7

J. D. EVANS, 'Two Phases of Prehistoric Settlement in the Western Mediter, ranean', *Bulletin of the University of London Institute of Archaeology, 1955–56*, 1958, pp. 1–22

Annual Reports of the Valletta Museum, from 1904 onwards

Sources of the Illustrations

The photographs for Plates 2, 13 and 17 were taken by the Helicopter Flight of H.M.S. *Falcon*. Of the remainder, those for Plates 4, 34, 35, 44, 51, 52, 61, 62, 64–74, 77, 81–5 and 87 are by W. Flores, those for Plates 53, 54, 63, 88–91, 96, 97 by Major Rickman, those for Plates 14, 15, 20–2, 27, 76 and 92 by the Author and the remainder are from negatives in the National Museum, Malta.

Figures 1, 13–15, 17 and 20 were drawn for this book by Mr C. G. Zammit, Director of the National Museum, Valletta; Figure 19 was drawn by Professor Stuart Piggott, and Figure 25 by Mr G. R. H. Wright. The rest were adapted from previous publications, with the exception of Figures 12, 21, 22, 24 and 26–8, which are the Author's.

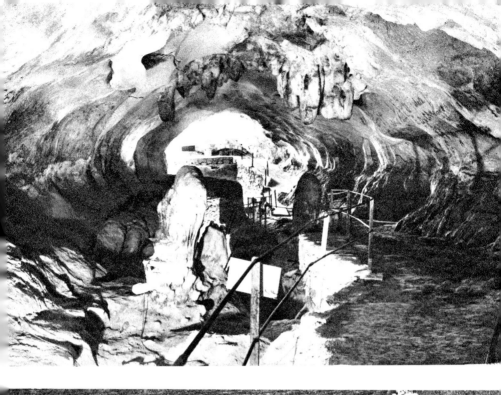

3

7

10

11

14

15

6

18

19

21

22

23

29

30

32

a

b

c

d

e

f

34

a

b

c

d

e

f

5

36

37 38

39

40

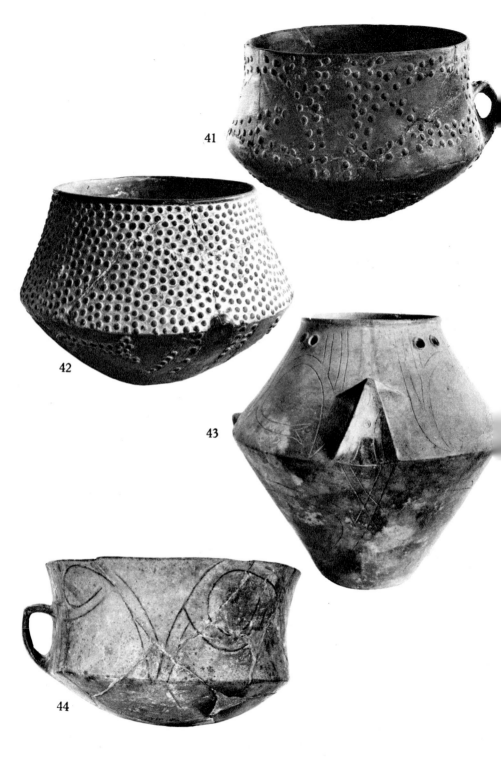

41

42

43

44

45

46

47

48

49

50

51   52

53

54

55

56

57

58

59

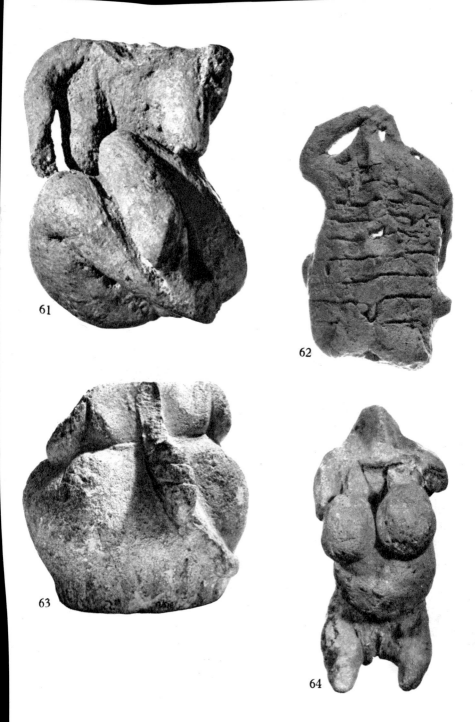

61

62

63

64

66

67

69

70

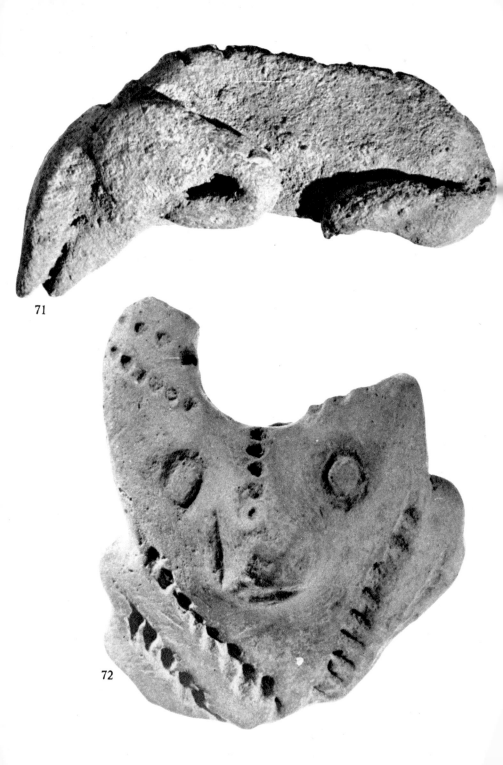

71

72

73

74

75

76

77

78

79

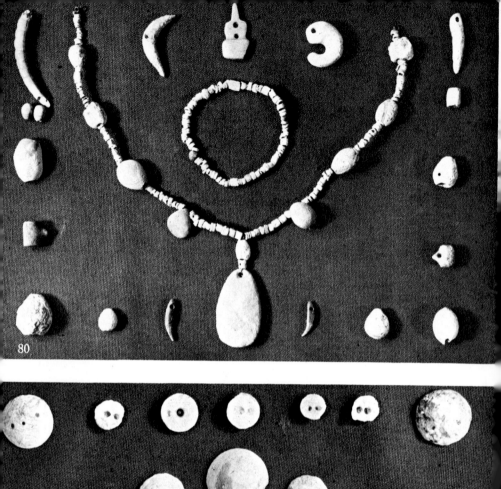

80

81

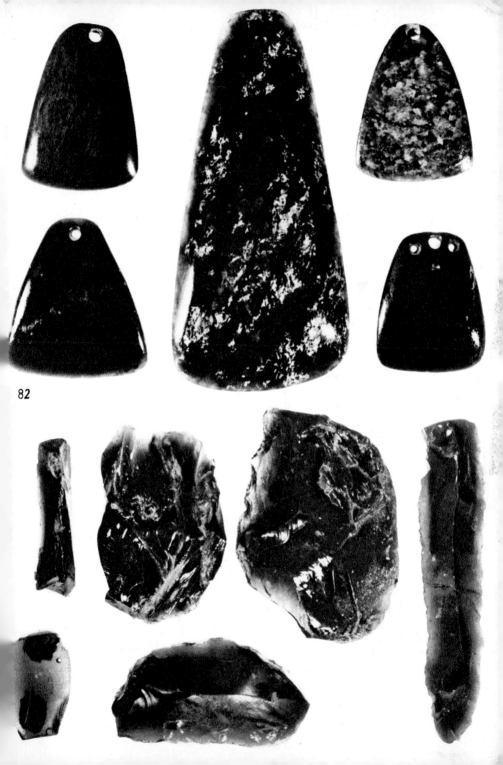

82

84

85

86

87

88

89

90

91

92

93

94

95

96

97

1 Għar Dalam (Dalam Cave). The interior, looking towards the entrance.

2 Ta Ħaġrat, Mġarr. Aerial view from the N.E. side. The earlier building is in the foreground.

3 Portion of a terracotta model representing the unroofed chamber of a temple. From Ħaġar Qim.

4 Left-hand chamber of the larger building at Ta Ħaġrat, Mġarr.

5 The façade of the southern temple of the Ġgantija.

6 The Ġgantija from the south.

7 The first chamber on the right in the southern temple of the Ġgantija; photograph of a painting made by H. Brocktorff in 1827, just after the excavation of the building.

8 The same chamber as it appears today.

9 The second chamber on the left and part of the rear chamber of the southern building of the Ġgantija.

10 View along the axis of the northern temple of the Ġgantija from the entrance.

11 The rear wall of the Ġgantija from the north.

12 The partially reconstructed façade of the Ħaġar Qim temples.

13 Aerial view of the Ħaġar Qim temples from the north.

14 The entrance to the first chamber on the right at Ħaġar Qim. Height of doorway 47 in.

15 The second chamber on the right at Ḣaġar Qim. Height of walls about 8 ft.

16 Ḣaġar Qim. View along the corridor which runs at right‑angles to the main axis and leads to the supplementary rooms. Note the mushroom‑shaped altars and the pitted decoration on the stones behind.

17 Aerial view of the Mnajdra temples from the south.

18 Corridor leading from the first to the second set of chambers in the southern temple at Mnajdra. Note the 'altars' flanking the entrance to the corridor.

19 Elaborately decorated entrance to the 'chamber of the pillar niches' in the southern temple at Mnajdra. The pittings have been made with a drill.

20 Part of the first chamber on the right in the southern temple at Mnajdra, showing the entrance to the small chamber between the walls, and the courses of corbelled blocks above. Height of doorway 41 in.

21 The first chamber on the right of the northern temple at Mnajdra. Note the much smaller dimensions of the slabs and blocks. Height of walls about 6 ft.

22 The first chamber on the right in the southern temple at Mnajdra, showing the rectangular opening communicating with the 'oracle chamber' behind the wall. Note the well‑preserved corbelling. Greatest height of walls about 13 ft.

23 The first chamber on the left of the western temple at Tarxien. The carvings shown here are reproductions of the originals placed there to protect them from weathering.

24 Photograph showing the originals of the carvings that appear on the left‑hand side of Plate 23, taken before they were covered.

25 The rear chamber and niche of the western temple at Tarxien. The carvings are the originals. Photograph taken before they were covered up.

26 The central part of the outer room of the middle temple at Tarxien, showing the partially blocked passage to the inner rooms.

27 Cutting made during the 1954 campaign in the second chamber on the right of the eastern temple at Tarxien, showing the way in which the rock-floor was hollowed out and the two superimposed *torba* floors.

28 Second chamber on the left of the middle temple at Tarxien, showing one of the carved stone screens (original).

29 One of the main halls of the Hal Saflieni Hypogeum. Note the ela-borately carved imitation of the façade of a megalithic building. The doorway in the centre leads to the chamber illustrated in the next plate.

30 Hal Saflieni Hypogeum. Elaborately carved chamber which leads to the 'Holy of Holies'. Note the imitation of corbelled masonry on the ceiling, and in the floor the two openings of a 'rope-hole' with their stone plugs.

31 Hal Saflieni Hypogeum. Hall with ceiling painted in red. The small recess in the wall on the right is popularly known as the 'oracle'.

32 The entrance to tombs 1 and 2 at Xemxija. Diameter of left-hand entrance about 39 in.

33 Interior of tomb 1 at Xemxija, showing two of the 'pilasters'. Height of nearest 'pilasters' about 51 in.

34 Fragments of pottery with simple impressed patterns, mostly done with a stick or finger nail.

35 Fragments of pottery with more elaborate impressed decoration, some of it done with a shell edge.

36 Flat-bottomed bowls from Żebbuġ: $1\frac{5}{8}$ in. deep (from tomb 2), $2\frac{1}{2}$ in. deep (from tomb 3).

37   Pot decorated in style of phase IC. Find spot unknown. Height 6 in.

38   Jar with anthropomorphic decoration datable to phase IC. Find spot unknown. From the collection of Chev. Dr J. G. Baldacchino. Height 10 in.

39   Biconical bowl from the Tarxien temples, decorated with scratched volute patterns. Height $4\frac{1}{8}$ in.

40   Carinated bowl, of type sometimes called a 'hanging bowl', current at the transition from phase ID to phase IE, with scratched decoration arranged in metopes. From the Hal Saflieni Hypogeum. Height 9 in.

41   Carinated bowl with decoration of applied studs. From the Tarxien temples. Height 9 in.

42   Carinated bowl from the Tarxien temples decorated with applied studs and white paste inlay. Height $6\frac{1}{8}$ in.

43   Large biconical jar with massive triangular handle. The four tunnel-lugs below the rim were probably intended for securing a cover. From the Tarxien temples. This is the largest pot ever found whole and undamaged on a Maltese site. Height 20 in.

44   Carinated bowl of a type probably used to contain food-offerings. There are plentiful traces of the incrustation of red ochre on this vessel which was held in place by the scratched lines. From the Tarxien temples. Height $5\frac{1}{2}$ in.

45   Large storage jar decorated with overlapping scales. From the Tarxien temples. Height $22\frac{1}{2}$ in.

46   Large 'amphora' with two tunnel-handles from the Tarxien temples. Height 19 in.

47   Small storage jar with a combination of applied, incised and fingertip decoration. From the Tarxien temples. Height 10 in.

48   Head of crude limestone statue from tomb 5 at Zebbuġ. Height $7\frac{3}{4}$ in.

Notes on the Plates

49 Headless standing figure in limestone from the Ħaġar Qim temples. Discovered recently with several others in circumstances which suggested that they had been found by earlier excavators and reinterred by them. Height 19 in.

50 Headless standing figure in limestone from the Hal Saflieni Hypogeum. Height 15½ in.

51, 52 Two small alabaster figurines from the Hal Saflieni Hypogeum. Height 2½ in.

53 Seated limestone figure from the Ħaġar Qim temples. Height 9¼ in.

54 Seated limestone figure clothed in a gown from the Ħaġar Qim temples. Height 9¼ in.

55, 56 Two limestone heads from the Hal Saflieni Hypogeum. Height 3¾ in. (left-hand example), 4¼ in. (right-hand example).

57 The 'Sleeping Lady' from the Hal Saflieni Hypogeum. Terracotta model representing a woman, clothed from the waist down in a fringed skirt, and reclining on a couch, her head resting on a pillow. Length 4⅝ in.

58, 59 Front and side views of the head of a large figurine of lightly baked clay found in the Tarxien temples. Height 4½ in.

60 Reconstruction of the complete figure, of which the head in the previous illustration forms a part. The skirt and left arm were reconstructed from fragments found with the head. The upper part of the body and the right arm are modern plaster. The height of the complete figure was probably about 24 in.

61 Tiny, roughly modelled figure from the Tarxien temples. Height 1¼ in.

62 Back view of a similar figurine from the Tarxien temples. In this case, in addition to the deformity, a number of sharp splinters of shell have been stuck into the clay. Height 2¾ in.

63 Headless, seated statuette of limestone with the remains of a long pigtail hanging down at the back. From Haġar Qim. Height $7\frac{1}{2}$ in.

64 Schematized and deformed female figure, perhaps representing a pathological condition. From the Mnajdra temples. Height 2 in.

65 The 'Venus of Malta'. A terracotta female torso from the Haġar Qim temples. Height 5 in.

66 Head from the Tarxien temples. Height 1 in.

67 Limestone head from the Tarxien temples. Height $1\frac{3}{8}$ in.

68 Stone head from the Tarxien temples. Height $1\frac{1}{4}$ in.

69 Head carved out of knob of stalactite embedded in limestone. From the Tarxien temples. Height of head 1 in.

70 Head with backward-sloping face, bull-neck and pigtail at back. The nose has been damaged and the figure is broken off at the shoulder. From the Tarxien temples. Height $1\frac{3}{4}$ in.

71 Rough terracotta figure of a lizard. From the Tarxien temples. Length $1\frac{3}{8}$ in.

72 Broken handle of vase in the form of an animal head. From Għar Dalam. Height $2\frac{3}{4}$ in.

73 Sherd of pottery with decoration in relief representing a bird (partridge?) set between a pair of horns. From the Tarxien temples. Height $1\frac{1}{2}$ in.

74 Fragment of a pottery bowl with incised repeat pattern consisting of three rows of crested birds in flight. From the Ġgantija. Height about 3 in.

75 Interior of shallow plate decorated with figures of humped cattle and goats. From the Hal Saflieni Hypogeum. Diameter 10 in.

76   Relief-carving on an upright slab of globigerina limestone in the northern temple at Mnajdra, which appears to represent a small megalithic shrine. Height $9\frac{1}{2}$ in.

77   Small limestone model of a megalithic shrine whose plan resembles that of the earliest surviving building in Malta. Length $1\frac{3}{4}$ in.

78   Slab of globigerina limestone carved in relief with opposed spirals. This pattern may be intended to symbolize watchful eyes. Compare Plate 26. From the Haġar Qim temples. Height 17 in.

79   Elaborately carved block of stone with 'potted plant' pattern. From the Haġar Qim temples, where it formed part of ritual installation with the slab in the preceding illustration. Height $28\frac{3}{4}$ in.

80   Selection of beads and pendants from the Hal Saflieni Hypogeum. The bone pendant (top centre) is probably a stylized human figure. Height $1\frac{1}{2}$ in.

81   Shell buttons, some inlaid with pieces of dark greenstone, and a large shell pendant from the Hal Saflieni Hypogeum. Length $3\frac{1}{2}$ in.

82   Axe-pendants made from green igneous rocks. From the Hal Saflieni Hypogeum. Length of middle pendant $3\frac{3}{4}$ in.

83   Knife, flakes and blades of obsidian from the Tarxien temples. Length of knife (on right) $3\frac{3}{4}$ in.

84   Carefully worked cylindrical bead of hard greenstone. The engraved pattern, which is probably symbolic or talismanic, is inlaid with gold and precious stones. Diameter $\frac{5}{8}$ in.

85   Potsherd incised with sign similar to that which appears on the bead in the previous illustration. Breadth of sherd about $1\frac{3}{4}$ in.
Pebble pendant bearing an engraved sign like that on the preceding two objects. Height $1\frac{3}{8}$ in.
Potsherd with scratched decoration, which includes a 'double-axe' sign. Height 4 in.

86 Upper part of a large limestone basin with triangular handle, which imitates a popular pottery shape. From Haġar Qim. Diameter 31½ in.

87 Rough lump of limestone with small recess carved to imitate a niche of slabs. Inside, two phalli and a disk with a hole through the middle. From the Tarxien temples. Height 3½ in.

88 Decorated bowl from the cremation cemetery in the Tarxien temples. Height 3 in.

89 Stylized idol from the cremation cemetery in the Tarxien temples. Height 7 in.

90 Decorated jug from the cremation cemetery in the Tarxien temples. Height 3¾ in.

91 Stylized female idol from the cremation cemetery in the Tarxien temples. Height 8¾ in.

92 'Dolmen' of rough stones near Musta. Height about 6 ft.

93 Portion of the massive defensive wall across the landward side of the Borġ in-Nadur promontory. Height *c.* 12 ft.

94 Footed bowl reconstructed from portions of two separate vessels of approximately the same size. From Borġ in-Nadur. Height 8¾ in.

95 Handled bowl with axe-like projection standing up above the rim. From Borġ in-Nadur. Height (to tip of handle) 6⅝ in.

96 Base of bowl from Bahrija showing elaborate incised meander decoration. Diameter 6¼ in.

97 Body of broken jug from Bahrija showing incised meander and excised zig-zag patterns. Maximum diameter 3¼ in.

Index

Abela, Commendatore G. F. 18
Aegean 74, 82, 108, 138, 143, 162
Aesthetic sense 165–6
Africa 189
Agriculture 157
Altars 98–9, 108, 138
Anatolia 176
Ancestor cult 136, 138
Anghelu Ruju Cemetery, Sardinia 133
Apulia 74
Ashby, Dr Thomas 23, 51, 112, 120
Ausonian culture 187–8

Bahrija 24, 187–8, 190
Baldacchino, Dr J. G. 36
Balearic islands 134
Borġ, J. 35
Borġ in-Nadur 17, 20, 26, 125, 180, 182,
    184–7, 190
Bouverie, Sir H. 19
Bradley, H. N. 23
Brea, Dr Bernabò 184
Brocktorff 99
Bronze Age pottery 26
    weapons 24
Buġibba 27, 82, 125, 152, 157
Buqana 129
Bur Mgħez 129
Busbisija 129

Canale Ianchina 188
Capo Graziano ware 178, 179, 180
Carthaginians 24, 29, 188
Caruana, Dr A. A. 20, 98
Castelluccio 134
Ceschi, Carlo 126
Chalcolithic period 83
Ciantar, Count 18
Clans 167
Comino 31
Cominotto 31
Corbelling (false-vaulting) 126–7
Costume 161–2
Cremation graves at Tarxien 24, 178
Crete 38, 82, 162–3, 164
Cult figures 140–5, 152, 175–6
Cyclades 37, 45, 140, 176

'Diana' ware 65
'Dolmens' 176–7, 179

Elephants, dwarf 35
Evans, Sir Arthur 138, 163
Evans, Professor Ifor 28

Fenton, Captain E. G. 189
Fergusson, James 20

Index

Fertility deities 117, 136, 142, 144, 152, 167

Figures (naturalistic) 144–5, 146, 147, 148–9, 152–3, 160–1

Filfla 31, 109

Fishing 157

Fontbouïsse style pottery 83

France 73, 83, 91, 191

Ġgantija 18, 65, 72, 74, 96, 98, 101, 106, 107, 110, 111, 120, 122, 126, 134, 142, 151, 152, 155, 163, 182, 191, 192

Għar Dalam 21, 35, 36, 39, 44, 53, 92, 151

Gozo 31, 51, 62, 182

Gracie, Captain H. S. 189–90

Graffiti 116

Greece 38, 45, 73, 143, 162–4, 191

Guardia ta San Gorg 182

Habitations 156–7

Haeduus, Quintinus 17

Ħaġar Qim 18, 19, 21, 23, 72, 85, 103–12, 114, 119, 122, 126, 137, 138, 139, 143, 149, 163, 192

Hal Ġinwi 125, 151

Hal Saflieni, Hypogeum of 22–3, 36, 52, 72, 75, 82, 84, 85, 91, 92, 107, 108, 127, 129, 131–3, 137, 140, 142, 143, 147, 148, 151, 152, 153, 155, 157, 160, 163, 191

Helbaek, Dr 173

Hepworth, Barbara 166

Hippopotami 35, 36

Houel, Jean 18

Hunting 157

Id-Debdieba 26

Id-Dura tal Mara 177

Impressed pottery, 41 44–5

Incubation 153, 163

In-Nuffara 182

Italy 73, 83, 160, 179, 186

Keith, Sir Arthur 36

Knossos 148

Kordin 20, 51, 53, 68, 72, 95, 96, 192

Lecce 179

Levy, R. 142

Liguria 160

Limestone 32, 33
    Coralline 33–4, 94, 109
    Globigerina 33–4, 105, 106, 126, 128, 132

Li Skorba 94

Louis XVI of France 18

Magri, Fr E. 22

Marfa 192

Marmora, Alberto de la 18

Marsaxlokk 17, 182

Mayr, Albert 22, 111, 138

Mazzara, L. 18

Mdina 156

Megalithic temples 48, 51, 52, 84, 155–6

Megaliths 24–5
Mġarr 26–7, 51, 52, 53, 62, 65, 85–6, 90, 91, 92, 95, 96, 100, 112, 126, 127, 134, 137, 149, 159, 192
Miocene period 32
Misrah Sinjura 177
Mnajdra 19, 23, 82, 109, 113–14, 120, 122, 124, 127, 137, 149, 151, 192
Monte Finocchito 185
Moore, Henry 166
Mtarfa 181
Murray, Dr Margaret 26, 182

Nadur 129
Neanderthal man 36, 39
Neolithic colonists 37, 166
Newton, Sir Charles 21

Ochre 135
Oligocene period 32
Orkney 91
Otrante 179

Pawla 191–2
Peet, T. E. 23, 52, 187
Phoenicians 20, 22
Portugal 83

Qrendi 101, 192

Religious rites 90–1, 121, 124, 131, 135–9, 154
Rock-cut tombs 48, 51, 52, 89, 92, 129, 135, 156
Rope-holes 136–7

Sacrifices of animals 116, 138–9
St George's Bay 182
St John, Knights of 18
San Cono style pottery 63, 159
San Ippolito culture, Sicily 81
Santa Verna 23
Santa Verna temple, Gozo 65, 86
Sardinia 73, 161
Sicily 25, 44–5, 54, 134, 136, 160, 184, 185, 186, 189, 191
'Sleeping Lady' 145–6, 153, 163, 166
Slide-car 190
Spain 83, 134, 160
Spirits of the dead 136, 137
Statue-menhirs 66
Stentinello type pottery 45, 53–4, 63, 64

Taboos 156
Tagliaferro, Professor N. 23, 52
Ta Ħaġrat 26
Tal Qadi 27, 124
Tarxien 24, 72, 82, 85, 96, 106, 107, 111, 113–14, 117, 118, 122, 124, 128, 137, 140, 144, 145, 148, 149, 151, 156, 157, 160, 162, 163, 169, 191
Tarxien Cemetery culture 169, 172, 175, 177–80, 183, 187
Temenos 134
Temple-culture 26
Tethys sea 34
Trade 160–1

Ugolini 27, 84

Index

Valletta, National Museum 191
Vance, J. G. 19
Vassallo, C. 20
'Venus of Malta' 146–7, 166
Victoria, Public Library 191

Ward Perkins, J. B. 182
Weapons 157–8
Wied Moqbol 177
Woolner, Mrs D. 116

Xagħra 18, 182
Xemxija 52, 68, 70, 73, 89, 90, 91, 129, 130, 133, 159
Xewkija 23, 52, 86
Xrobb il-Għaġin 26, 125

Zammit, Sir Themistocles 17, 23, 24, 25, 84, 103, 113, 115, 121, 123, 137, 151, 153, 158, 168, 173, 189, 190
Zebbuġ 60, 62–3, 65, 129, 136, 159, 160

Date Due

JUN 2 2 '60			
JUL 7 '60			
Reserve			
OCT 6 '64			
GB	PRINTED IN U. S. A.		